Tipping recommendations

KV-028-813

Obviously, tipping is an individual matter, and the correct amount to leave varies enormously with category of hotel or restaurant, size of city and so on. The sums we suggest represent normal tips for average middle-grade establishments in big cities.

	Italy	Switzerland
HOTEL		
Service charge, bill	15–20% (included)	15% (included)
Porter, per bag	L. 500	1 Fr.
Bellboy, errand	L. 1.000	1 Fr.
Maid, per week	L. 5.000–7.000	10 Fr.
Doorman, hails cab	L. 500–1.000	1 Fr.
RESTAURANT		
Service charge, bill	12–15% (included)	15% (included)
Waiter	10%	optional
Hat check	L. 500	1 Fr.
Lavatory attendant	L. 300	50 ct.
Taxi driver	15%	15% (sometimes incl.)
Barber/Women's hairdresser	15%	10–15% (included)
Theatre usher	L. 500	–
Tour guide	10%	optional

BERLITZ PHRASE BOOKS

World's bestselling phrase books feature not only expressions and vocabulary you'll need, but also travel tips, useful facts and pronunciation throughout. The handiest and most readable conversation aid available.

Arabic	French	Portuguese
Chinese	German	Russian
Danish	Greek	Serbo-Croatian
Dutch	Hebrew	Spanish
European	Hungarian	Latin-American
(14 languages)	Italian	Spanish
European	Japanese	Swahili
Menu Reader	Norwegian	Swedish
Finnish	Polish	Turkish

BERLITZ CASSETTEPAKS

The above-mentioned titles are also available combined with a cassette to help you improve your accent. A helpful 32-page script is included containing the complete text of the dual language hi-fi recording.

BERLITZ®

ITALIAN
FOR TRAVELLERS

By the staff of Editions Berlitz

Copyright © 1970, 1974 by Editions Berlitz, a division of Macmillan S.A.

All rights reserved. No part of this book may be reproduced or transmitted in any form or by any means, electronic or mechanical, including photocopying, recording or by any information storage and retrieval system, without permission in writing from the Publisher.

Library of Congress Catalog Card Number: 74-1977

Revised edition
24th printing 1985

Printed in Hungary

Berlitz Trademark Reg. U.S. Patent Office
and other countries—Marca Registrada

Editions Berlitz
1, avenue des Jordils
1000 Lausanne 6, Switzerland

Preface

In preparing this book we took into account a wealth of suggestions from phrase book users around the world. The accent is on helping the traveller in practical, every-day situations.

The contents are logically arranged so you can find the right phrase at the moment you need it.

Italian for Travellers features:

● all the phrases and supplementary vocabulary you'll need on your trip

● complete phonetic transcription throughout, enabling you to pronounce every word correctly

● special panels showing replies your listener might like to give you: just hand him the book and let him point to the appropriate phrase. This is particularly useful in certain difficult situations (trouble with the car, at the doctor's, etc.)

● a wide range of travel facts, hints and useful practical information

● a tipping chart (see inside back-cover) and a reference section in the back of the book

● an introduction to some basics of Italian grammar

These are just a few of the practical advantages. In addition, the book will prove a valuable introduction to life in Italy and Switzerland.

There's a comprehensive section on Eating Out, giving translations and explanations for practically anything one would find on an Italian menu; there's a complete Shopping Guide that will enable you to obtain virtually anything you want. Trouble with the car? Turn to the mechanic's manual with its dual-language terms. Feeling ill? Our medical section provides the most rapid communication possible between you and the doctor.

To make the most of *Italian for Travellers*, we suggest that you start with the "Guide to Pronunciation". Then go on to "Some Basic Expressions". This not only gives you a minimum vocabulary; it helps you to pronounce the language.

We're particularly grateful to Mrs. Francesca Rahimi and Dr. Giannino Rigolio for their help in the preparation of this book and to Dr. T.J.A. Bennett who devised the phonetic transcription. We also wish to thank the Italian Government Travel Office for its assistance.

We shall be very pleased to receive any comments, criticisms and suggestions that you think may help us in preparing future editions.

Thank you. Have a good trip.

Throughout this book, the symbols illustrated here indicate small sections where phrases have been compiled that your foreign listener might like to say to *you*. If you don't understand him, give him the book and let him point at the phrase in his language. The English translation is just beside it.

A very basic grammar

Articles

There are two genders in Italian – masculine (masc.) and feminine (fem.).

1. *Definite article* (the):

masc. (sing.)	(plur.)
l' before a vowel	gli
lo before z or s + consonant	gli
il before all other consonants	i

l'amico (the friend)	gli amici (the friends)
lo studente (the student)	gli studenti (the students)
il treno (the train)	i treni (the trains)

fem. (sing.)	(plur.)
l' before a vowel	le
la before a consonant	le

l'arancia (the orange)	le arance (the oranges)
la casa (the house)	le case (the houses)

2. *Indefinite article* (a/an):

masc.: un/uno before z or s + consonant*

un magazzino	a department store
uno stadio	a stadium

fem.: una/un' before a vowel

una strada	a street
un'amica	a girl friend

3. *Partitive* (some/any):

In affirmative sentences and some interrogatives, **some** and **any** are expressed by **di** + definite article, which has the following contracted forms:

masc. (sing.)	(plur.)
dell' before a vowel	degli
dello before z or s + consonant	degli
del before other consonants	dei

---

* When s is followed by a vowel, the masculine articles are il/i (definite) and un (indefinite).

GRAMMAR

GRAMMAR

fem. (sing.)	(plur.)
dell' before a vowel	**delle**
della before a consonant	**delle**

For other contractions of preposition + definite article, see page 11.

Desidero del vino.	I want some wine.
Vorrei delle sigarette.	I'd like some cigarettes.
Hai degli amici a Roma?	Have you any friends in Rome?

Nouns

Nouns ending in **o** are generally masculine. To form the plural, change **o** to **i**.

il tavolo (the table) **i tavoli** (the tables)

Nouns ending in **a** are usually feminine. To form the plural, change **a** to **e**.

la casa (the house) **le case** (the houses)

Nouns ending in **e**—no rule as to gender. Learn each noun individually. Plurals are formed by changing the **e** to **i**.

il piede (the foot) **i piedi** (the feet)
la notte (the night) **le notti** (the nights)

Adjectives

They agree with the noun they modify in number and gender. There are two basic types—ending in **o** and ending in **e**.

masc. (sing.)	(plur.)
leggero light (in weight)	**leggeri**
grande big	**grandi**
fem. (sing.)	(plur.)
leggera	**leggere**
grande	**grandi**

They usually follow the noun but certain common adjectives precede the noun.

un caro amico a dear friend
una strada lunga a long street

Demonstratives

this	**questo/questa** (contracted to **quest'** before a vowel)
these	**questi/queste** (no contraction)

That/these: follow same system as **dell'/dello/della,** etc.

| that | (masc.) **quell', quello, quel/**(fem.) **quell', quella** |
| these | (masc.) **quegli, quei/**(fem.) **quelle** |

Possessive adjectives and pronouns

These agree in number and gender *with the nouns they modify* (or replace). They are almost always used with the definite article.

	Masculine		Feminine	
	singular	plural	singular	plural
my, mine	**il mio**	**i miei**	**la mia**	**le mie**
your, yours	**il tuo**	**i tuoi**	**la tua**	**le tue**
his, her, hers, its	**il suo**	**i suoi**	**la sua**	**le sue**
our, ours	**il nostro**	**i nostri**	**la nostra**	**le nostre**
your, yours	**il vostro**	**i vostri**	**la vostra**	**le vostre**
their, theirs	**il loro**	**i loro**	**la loro**	**le loro**
*your, yours (sing.)	**il suo**	**i suoi**	**la sua**	**le sue**
*your, yours (plur.)	**il loro**	**i loro**	**la loro**	**le loro**

Thus, depending on the context:

| **il suo cane** | can mean | his, her, your dog |
| **la sua auto** | can mean | his, her, your car |

Personal pronouns

	Subject	Direct Object	Indirect Object	After a Preposition
I	**io**	**mi**	**mi**	**me**
you	**tu**	**ti**	**ti**	**te**
he, it (masc.)	**lui, egli**	**lo**	**gli**	**lui, esso**
she, it (fem.)	**lei, ella, essa**	**la**	**le**	**lei, essa**
we	**noi**	**ci**	**ci**	**noi**
you	**voi**	**vi**	**vi**	**voi**
they (masc.)	**loro, esse**	**li**	**loro**	**loro**
they (fem.)	**loro, esse**	**le**	**loro**	**loro**

* This is the formal form—used in addressing people you do not know well.

GRAMMAR

Note: There are two forms for "you" in Italian: **tu** (singular) is used when talking to relatives, close friends and children (and between young people); the plural of **tu** is **voi**. **Lei** is used in all other cases (with the 3rd person singular of the verb).

Verbs

Learn these two auxiliary verbs:

Infinitive:	
essere (to be)	**avere** (to have)
Present tense:	
io* sono (I am)	io ho (I have)
tu sei (you are)	tu hai (you have)
lui, lei è (he, she, it is)	lui, lei ha (he, she, it has)
lei è (you are)	lei ha (you have)
noi siamo (we are)	noi abbiamo (we have)
voi siete (you are)	voi avete (you have)
essi sono (they are)	essi hanno (they have)

Regular verbs follow one of three patterns:

	ends in -are	ends in -ere	ends in -ire
Infinitive:	**comprare** (to buy)	**vendere** (to sell)	**partire** (to leave)
Present tense:			
io	compro	vendo	parto
tu	compri	vendi	parti
lui, lei	compra	vende	parte
noi	compriamo	vendiamo	partiamo
voi	comprate	vendete	partite
essi	comprano	vendono	partono

---

* The subject pronouns are seldom used except for emphasis.

Here are four useful irregular verbs:

Infinitive:	**andare** (to go)	**potere** (to be able)	**vedere** (to see)	**fare** (to make)
io	vado	posso	vedo	faccio
tu	vai	puoi	vedi	fai
lui, lei	va	può	vede	fa
noi	andiamo	possiamo	vediamo	facciamo
voi	andate	potete	vedete	fate
essi	vanno	possono	vedono	fanno

Negatives

Negatives are formed by putting **non** before the verb.

Non vado a Roma.   I am not going to Rome.

Questions

In Italian, questions are often formed by simply changing the inflexion of your voice. Remember that the personal pronoun is rarely used, either in affirmative sentences or in questions.

Parlo italiano.   I speak Italian.
Parla italiano?   Do you speak Italian?

Prepositions

There is a list of prepositions on page 21. Note the following contractions.

Definite Article	**a** at, to	**da** by, from	**di** of	**in** in	**su** on	**con** with
+il	al	dal	del	nel	sul	col
+l'	all'	dall'	dell'	nell'	sull'	con l'
+lo	allo	dallo	dello	nello	sullo	con lo
+la	alla	dalla	della	nella	sulla	con la
+i	ai	dai	dei	nei	sui	coi/con i
+gli	agli	dagli	degli	negli	sugli	con gli
+le	alle	dalle	delle	nelle	sulle	con le

GRAMMAR

Guide to pronunciation

This and the following chapter are intended to make you familiar with the phonetic transcription we devised and to help you get used to the sounds of Italian.

As a minimum vocabulary for your trip, we've selected a number of basic words and phrases under the title "Some Basic Expressions" (pages 15–21).

An outline of the spelling and sounds of Italian

You'll find the pronunciation of the Italian letters and sounds explained below, as well as the symbols we're using for them in the transcriptions. Note that Italian has some diacritical letters—letters with accent marks—which we don't use in English.

The imitated pronunciation should be read as if it were English except for any special rules set out below. It is based on Standard British pronunciation, though we have tried to take account of General American pronunciation also. Of course, the sounds of any two languages are never exactly the same; but if you follow carefully the indications supplied here, you'll have no difficulty in reading our transcriptions in such a way as to make yourself understood.

Letters written in **bold** should be stressed (pronounced louder).

Consonants

Letter	Approximate pronunciation	Symbol	Example
b, d, f, k, l, m, n, p, q, t, v	are pronounced as in English		

PRONUNCIATION

c	1) before **e** and **i**, like **ch** in **chip**	ch	**cerco**	chayrkoa
	2) elsewhere, like **c** in **cat**	k	**conto**	koantoa
ch	like **c** in **cat**	k	**che**	kay
g	1) before **e** and **i**, like **j** in **jet**	j	**valigia**	vahleejah
	2) elsewhere, like **g** in **go**	g	**grande**	grahnday
gh	like **g** in **go**	g	**ghiaccio**	geeahtchoa
gl	like **lli** in **million**	ly	**gli**	lyee
gn	like **ni** in **onion**	ñ	**bagno**	bahñoa
h	always silent		**ha**	ah
r	trilled like a Scottish **r**	r	**deriva**	dehreevah
s	1) generally like **s** in **sit**	s/ss	**questo** **casa**	kooaystoa karssah
	2) sometimes like **z** in **zoo**	z	**viso**	veezoa
sc	1) before **e**, **i**, like **sh** in **shut**	sh	**uscita**	oosheetah
	2) elsewhere, like **sk** in **skin**	sk	**scarpa**	skahrpah
z or **zz**	1) generally like **ts** in **hits**	ts	**grazie**	grartseeay
	2) sometimes like **ds** in **roads**	dz	**romanzo**	roamahndzoa

Vowels

a	1) short, like **ar** in **car**, but shorter	ah	**gatto**	gahttoa
	2) long, like **ar** in **car**	ar*	**casa**	karssah
e	1) can always be pronounced like **ay** in **way**	ay	**sera**	sayrah
	2) in correct speech, it is sometimes pronounced like **e** in **get** or, when long, more like **air** in **hair**	eh ai	**bello** **bene**	behlloa bainay
i	like **ee** in **meet**	ee	**vini**	veenee

---

* The r should not be pronounced when reading this transcription.

o	1) can always be pronounced like **oa** in g**oa**t	oa	**sole**	**soa**lay
	2) in correct speech, it is sometimes pronounced like **o** in g**o**t, or when long, more like **aw** in l**aw**	o	**notte**	**not**tay
		aw	**rosa**	**raw**zah
u	like **oo** in f**oo**t	oo	**fumo**	**foo**moa

Two or more vowels

In groups of vowels **a**, **e**, and **o** are strong vowels, and **i** and **u** are weak vowels. When two strong vowels are next to each other, they are pronounced as two separate syllabes, e.g., *beato* = bay**ah**toa. When a strong and weak vowel are next to each other, the weak one is pronounced more quickly and with less stress (less loudly) than the strong one, e.g., *piede* = pee**ay**day; such sounds are diphthongs and constitute only one syllable. If the weak vowel is stressed, then it is pronounced as a separate syllable, e.g., *due* = **doo**ay. Two weak vowels together are pronounced as a diphthong, and it is generally the second one that is more strongly stressed, e.g., *guida* = goo**ee**dah.

Stressing of words

Generally, the vowel of the next to the last syllable is stressed. When a final vowel is stressed, it has an accent written over it *(più)*. Normally an accent is used only when the stress falls on a final vowel, and not when it falls on syllables before the next to the last one.

PRONUNCIATION

Some basic expressions

Yes.	**Sì.**	see
No.	**No.**	no
Please.	**Per piacere.**	pair peeah**chay**ray
Thank you.	**Grazie.**	**grart**seeay
Thank you very much.	**Molte grazie.**	**moal**tay **grart**seeay
	Tante grazie.	**tahn**tay **grart**seeay
That's all right.	**Va bene.**	vah **bai**nay
You're welcome.	**Prego.**	**pray**goa

Greetings

Good morning.	**Buongiorno.**	bwon**joar**noa
Good afternoon.	**Buongiorno.**	bwon**joar**noa
Good evening.	**Buona sera.**	**bwo**nah **say**rah
Good night.	**Buona notte.**	**bwo**nah **not**tay
Good-bye.	**Arrivederci.**	ahrreevay**dair**chee
So long!	**Ciao!**	**cha**roa
See you later.	**A più tardi.**	ah **pee**oo **tahr**dee
This is Mr. ...	**Le presento il signor...**	lay pray**zayn**toa eel see**ñoar**
This is Mrs. ...	**Le presento la signora...**	lay pray**zayn**toa lah see**ñoa**rah
This is Miss...	**Le presento la signorina...**	lay pray**zayn**toa lah seeñoa**ree**nah

How do you do?	**Molto lieto.**	moaltoa leeaytoa
I'm very pleased to meet you.	**Sono molto lieto di fare la sua conoscenza.**	soanoa moaltoa leeaytoa dee farray lah sooah koanoashehntsah
How are you?	**Come sta?**	koamay stah
Very well, thanks.	**Molto bene, grazie.**	moaltoa bainay grartseeay
And you?	**E lei?**	ay laiee
How's it going?	**Come va?**	koamay vah
Excuse me. (I didn't hear.)	**Mi scusi.**	mee skoozee
Excuse me. (May I get past?)	**Permesso?**	pairmaisssoa
That's all right.	**Non importa.**	noan eemportah
I beg your pardon?	**Come dice?**	koamay deechay

Questions

Where?	**Dove?**	doavay
Where is...?	**Dov'è...?**	doavai
Where are...?	**Dove sono...?**	doavay soanoa
When?	**Quando?**	kwahndoa
What?	**Che cosa/Che?**	kay kawssah/kay
How?	**Come?**	koamay
How much?	**Quanto?**	kwahntoa
How many?	**Quanti?**	kwahntee
Who?	**Chi?**	kee
Why?	**Perchè?**	pehrkay
Which?	**Quale?**	kwarlay

What do you call this in Italian?	**Come si chiama questo in italiano?**	koamay see keearmah kooaystoa een eetahleearnoa
What do you call that in Italian?	**Come si chiama quello in Italiano?**	koamay see keearmah kooaylloa een eetahleearnoa
What do you call these in Italian?	**Come si chiamano questi in italiano?**	koamay see keearmahnoa kooaystee een eetahleearnoa
What does this mean?	**Che cosa significa questo?**	kay kawssah seeñeefeekah kooaystoa
What does that mean?	**Che cosa significa quello?**	kay kawssah seeñeefeekah kooaylloa

Do you speak...?

Do you speak...?	**Parla...?**	pahrlah
Do you speak English?	**Parla inglese?**	pahrlah eengglayssay
Is there anyone here who speaks...?	**C'è qualcuno qui che parla...?**	chai kwahlkoonoa kooee kay pahrlah
I don't speak much Italian.	**Non parlo bene l'italiano.**	noan pahrloa bainay leetahleearnoa
Could you speak more slowly?	**Può parlare più lentamente, per favore?**	pwo pahrlarray peeoo layntahmayntay pair fahvoaray
Could you repeat that?	**Vuol ripetere, per favore?**	vwol reepaitayray pair fahvoaray
Please write it down.	**Per favore, me lo scriva.**	pair fahvoaray may loa skreevah
Can you translate this for me?	**Può tradurmi questo?**	pwo trahdoormee kooaystoa
Please point to the phrase in the book.	**Per favore, mi indichi la frase nel libro.**	pair fahvoaray mee eendeekee lah frarzay nehl leebroa
Just a minute. I'll see if I can find it in this book.	**Un attimo, per favore. Guardo se posso trovarla in questo libro.**	oon ahtteemoa pair fahvoaray. gwahrdoa say posssoa troavarrlah een kooaystoa leebroa

I understand.	Capisco.	kahpeeskoa
I don't understand.	Non capisco.	noan kahpeeskoa
Do you understand?	Capisce?	kahpeeshay

Can...?

Can I have...?	Posso avere...?	posssoa ahvayray
Can we have...?	Possiamo avere...?	posseearmoa ahvayray
Can you show me...?	Può mostrarmi...?	pwo moastrarrmee
I can't.	Non posso.	noan posssoa
Can you tell me...?	Può dirmi...?	pwo deermee
Can you help me?	Può aiutarmi?	pwo ighootarrmee
Can I help you?	Posso aiutarla?	posssoa ighootarrlah
Can you direct me to...?	Può indicarmi la direzione per...?	pwo eendeekahrmee lah deeraytseeoanay pair

Wanting

I'd like...	Vorrei...	vorraiee
We'd like...	Vorremmo...	vorrehmmoa
What do you want?	Che cosa desidera?	kay kawssah dayzeedayrah
Give me...	Mi dia...	mee deeah
Give it to me.	Me lo dia.	may loa deeah
Bring me...	Mi porti...	mee portee
Bring it to me.	Me lo porti.	may loa portee
Show me...	Mi mostri...	mee moastree
Show it to me.	Me lo mostri.	may loa moastree

I'm looking for...	Cerco...	chayrkoa
I'm hungry.	Ho fame.	oa farmay
I'm thirsty.	Ho sete.	oa saytay
I'm tired.	Sono stanco.	soanoa stahngkoa
I'm tired.*	Sono stanca.	soanoa stahngkah
I'm lost.	Mi sono perduto.	mee soanoa pehrdootoa
It's important.	È importante.	ai eemportahntay
It's urgent.	È urgente.	ai oorjehntay
Hurry up!	Presto!	prehstoa

It is/There is...

It is/It's...	È...	ai
Is it...?	È...?	ai
It isn't...	Non è...	noan ai
There it is.	Eccolo.	ehkkoaloa
There you are!	Eccoti!	ehkkoatee
Here they are.	Eccoli/Eccole.	ehkkoalee/ehkkoalay
There it is.	Eccolo.	ehkkoaloa
There they are.	Eccoli.	ehkkoalee
There is/There are...	Vi è/Vi sono...	vee ai/vee soanoa
Is there/Are there...?	C'é/Ci sono...?	chai/chee soanoa
There isn't/There aren't...	Non c'è/Non ci sono...	noan chai/noan chee soanoa
There isn't any.	Non ce n'è.	noan chay nai
There aren't any.	Non ce ne sono.	noan chay nay soanoa

* Said by a woman.

SOME BASIC EXPRESSIONS

It's...

big/small	**grande/piccolo**	grahnday/peekkoaloa
quick/slow	**rapido/lento**	rarpeedoa/lehntoa
early/late	**presto/tardi**	prehstoa/tahrdee
cheap/expensive	**buon mercato/caro**	bwawn mayrkahtoa/karroa
near/far	**vicino/lontano**	veecheenoa/lontarnoa
hot/cold	**caldo/freddo**	kahldoa/frayddoa
full/empty	**pieno/vuoto**	peeaynoa/vwawtoa
easy/difficult	**facile/difficile**	farcheelay/deeffeecheelay
heavy/light	**pesante/leggero**	payssahntay/laydjairoa
open/shut	**aperto/chiuso**	ahpehrtoa/keeoossoa
right/wrong	**giusto/sbagliato**	joostoa/zbahlyartoa
old/new	**vecchio/nuovo**	vehkkeeoa/nwawvoa
old/young	**anziano/giovane**	ahntseeahnoa/joavahnay
next/last	**prossimo/scorso**	prossseemoa/skorsoa
beautiful/ugly	**bello/brutto**	bailloa/broottoa
free (vacant)/occupied	**libero/occupato**	leebayroa/okkoopartoa
good/bad	**buono/cattivo**	bwawnoa/kahtteevoa
better/worse	**migliore/peggiore**	meelyoaray/paydjoaray
here/there	**qui/là**	kooee/lah
now/then	**adesso/dopo**	ardaisssoa/dawpoa

Quantities

a little/a lot	**un po'/molto**	oon po/moaltoa
much/many	**molto/molti**	moaltoa/moaltee
more than/less than	**più di/meno di**	peeooo dee/mainoa dee
enough/too	**abbastanza/troppo**	ahbbahstahntsa/troppoa
some (any)	**qualche**	kwahlkay

SOME BASIC EXPRESSIONS

A few prepositions and some more useful words

at	**a**	ah
on	**su**	soo
in	**in**	een
to	**a**	ah
from	**da**	dah
inside	**dentro**	dayntroa
outside	**fuori**	fwawree
up/upstairs	**su, in alto/di sopra**	soo een ahltoa/ dee **soa**prah
down/downstairs	**giù/di sotto**	joo/dee **soa**ttoa
for	**per**	payr
after	**dopo**	dawpoa
before (time)	**prima**	preemah
before (place)	**davanti**	dahvahntee
with	**con**	kon
without	**senza**	sayntsah
through	**per/attraverso**	pair/ahttrah**vehr**soa
towards	**verso**	vehrsoa
until	**fino a**	feenoa ah
during	**durante**	doorahntay
and	**e**	ay
or	**o**	oa
not	**non**	noan
nothing	**nulla/niente**	noollah/neeayntay
none	**nessuno**	naysssoonoa
very	**molto**	moaltoa
too (also)	**anche**	ahngkay
soon	**presto**	prehstoa
perhaps	**forse**	forsay

Arrival

You've arrived. Whether you've come by train, ship or plane, you'll have to go through passport and customs formalities. (For car/border control, see page 146.)

There's certain to be somebody around who speaks English. That's why we're making this a brief section. What you really want is to be off to your hotel in the shortest possible time. And here are the steps to get these formalities out of the way quickly.

Passport control

Here's my passport.	**Ecco il passaporto.**	ehkkoa eel pahsssahportoa
I'll be staying…	**Resterò…**	raystayroa
a few days	**qualche giorno**	kwahlkay joarnoa
a week	**una settimana**	oonah saytteemarnah
two weeks	**due settimane**	dooay saytteemarnay
a month	**un mese**	oon maizay
I don't know yet.	**Non so ancora.**	noan soa ahngkoarah
I'm here on holiday.	**Sono qui in vacanza.**	soanoa kooee een vahkahntsah
I'm here on business.	**Sono qui per affari.**	soanoa kooee pair ahffarree
I'm just passing through.	**Sono di passaggio.**	soanoa dee pahsssadjeeoa

If things become difficult:

I'm sorry, I don't understand.	**Mi dispiace, non capisco.**	mee deespeeahchay noan kahpeeskoa
Is there anyone here who speaks English?	**C'è qualcuno qui che parla inglese?**	chai kwahlkoonoa kooee kay pahrlah eengglayssay

Customs

The chart below shows what you can bring in duty-free (visitors from overseas are allowed greater concessions as regards duty-free cigarettes and tobacco).*

	Cigarettes		Cigars		Tobacco (grams)	Spirits (liquor) (lit.)		Wine (lit.)
Italy	300	or	75	or	400	1½	or	3
Switzerland	200	or	50	or	250	1	and	2

At almost all major airports in Europe, an honour system for clearing customs has been adopted. Baggage is often not even opened, although spot checks are a possibility. After collecting your baggage, you have a choice: follow the green arrow if you've nothing to declare. Or leave via a doorway marked with a red arrow if you've items to declare (in excess of those allowed).

MERCI DA DICHIARARE
GOODS TO DECLARE

NULLA DA DICHIARARE
NOTHING TO DECLARE

I've nothing to declare.	**Non ho nulla da dichiarare.**	noan oa **noo**llah dah deekeeah**r**rarray
I've a...	**Ho una...**	oa **oo**nah
carton of cigarettes	**stecca di sigarette**	**stay**kkah dee seegah**ray**ttay
bottle of whisky	**bottiglia di whisky**	bot**tee**lyah dee "whisky"
Must I pay on this?	**Devo pagare per questo?**	**day**voa pah**ga**rray pair **koo**aystoa
It's for my personal use.	**È per mio uso personale.**	ai pair **mee**oa **oo**zoa pair**soa**nar**lay**

---

* All allowances subject to change without notice.

Il passaporto, per favore.	Your passport, please.
Ha qualche cosa da dichiarare?	Do you have anything to declare?
Per favore, apra questa borsa.	Please open this bag.
Deve pagare il dazio per questo.	You'll have to pay duty on this.
Ha altri bagagli?	Do you have any more luggage?

Baggage—Porters

In the absence of porters, you'll find do-it-yourself luggage trolleys at the airport. You might find porters at the railway stations, but they are becoming scarce.

Where are the luggage trolleys?	**Dove sono i carrelli portabagagli?**	doavay soanoa ee kahrehllee portahbahgahlyee
Porter!	**Facchino!**	fahkkeenoa
Please take these bags.	**Per favore, prenda queste borse.**	pair fahvoaray prehndah kooaystay borsay
That's mine.	**Quella è la mia.**	kooayllah ai lah meeah
That's my...	**Quella è...**	kooayllah ai
bag	**la mia borsa**	lah meeah borsah
luggage	**il mio bagaglio**	eel meeoa bahgahlyoa
suitcase	**la mia valigia**	lah meeah vahleejah
That...one.	**Quella...**	kooayllah
big/small	**grande/piccola**	grahnday/peekkoalah
blue/brown	**blu/marrone**	bloo/mahrroanay
black/plaid	**nera/scozzese**	nayrah/skoattsayssay
There's one piece missing.	**Manca un collo.**	mahnkah oon kolloa
Take these bags to the...	**Porti queste borse...**	portee kooaystay borsay
bus	**all'autobus**	ahllowtoabooss
luggage lockers	**alla custodia automatica dei bagagli**	ahllah koostawdeeah owtoamarteekah daiee bahgarlyee

ARRIVAL

Changing money

You'll find a bank at most airports. If it's closed, don't worry. You'll be able to change money at your hotel.

Full details about money and currency exchange are given on pages 134–136.

Where's the nearest currency exchange?	Dove si trova l'ufficio cambio più vicino?	doavay see trawvah loofeecheeoa kahmbeeoa peeoo veecheenoa
Can you change these traveller's cheques (checks)?	Può cambiare questi traveller's cheques?	pwo kahmbeearray kooaystee "traveller's cheques"
I want to change some...	Vorrei cambiare...	vorraiee kahmbeearray
dollars	dei dollari	daiee dollahree
pounds	delle sterline	dayllay stayrleenay
Can you change this into lire?	Può cambiare questo in lire?	pwo kahmbeearray kooaystoa een leeray
What's the exchange rate?	Qual è il corso del cambio?	kwahl ai eel korsoa dayl kahmbeeoa

Directions

How do I get to...?	Come posso andare a...?	koamay posssoa ahndarray ah
Where's the bus to the centre of town?	Dov'è l'autobus che va in centro?	doavai lowtoabooss kay vah een chayntroa
Where can I get a taxi?	Dove posso prendere un taxi?	doavay posssoa prayndaray oon "taxi"
Where can I hire (rent) a car?	Dove posso noleggiare un'automobile?	doavay posssoa noalaydjeearray oonowtoamawbeelay

Hotel reservations

Many terminals have a hotel reservation service or tourist information office. You're sure to find someone there who speaks English. There's sometimes a special telephone that connects you to a hotel service or to individual hotels.

FOR NUMBERS, see page 176

ARRIVAL

Car rental

There are car rental firms at most airports and terminals.
It's highly likely that someone there will speak English. But
if nobody does, try one of the following:

I'd like a...	Vorrei noleggiare una...	vorraiee noalaydjeearray oonah
car	macchina	mahkkeenah
small car	macchina piccola	mahkkeenah peekkoalah
large car	macchina grande	mahkkeenah grahnday
sports car	macchina sportiva	mahkkeenah sporteevah
I'd like it for...	La vorrei per...	lah vorraiee pair
a day	un giorno	oon joarnoa
four days	quattro giorni	kwahttroa joarnee
a week	una settimana	oonah saytteemarnah
What's the charge per...?	Qual è la tariffa...?	kwahl ai lah tahreeffah
day	giornaliera	joarnahleeayrah
week	per una settimana	pair oona saytteemarnah
Does that include mileage?	Compreso il chilometraggio?	koampraysoa eel keelawmaytrahdjeeoa
What's the charge per kilometre?	Qual è la tariffa al chilometro?	kwahl ai lah tarreeffah ahl keelawmaytroa
Is petrol (gasoline) included?	È incluso il prezzo della benzina?	ai eengkloozoa eel prehtsoa dayllah bayndzeenah
I want full insurance.	Voglio l'assicurazione completa.	volyoa lahssseekooraht-seeoanay koamplaytah
What's the deposit?	Quanto è la cauzione?	kwahntoa ai lah kowtseeoanay
I've a credit card.	Ho una carta di credito.	oa oonah karrtah dee kraydeetoa
Here's my driving licence.	Ecco la mia patente.	ehkkoa lah meeah partehntay

FOR SIGHTSEEING, see page 75

Taxi

All taxis have meters. It's usually best to ask the approximate fare beforehand. For some trips (e.g., airport to town) there may be a fixed rate. This will be posted at the airport. From 10 p.m. to 7 a.m. there's a night supplement which isn't indicated on the meter.

Where can I get a taxi?	Dove posso trovare un taxi?	doavay posssoa trawvahray oon "taxi"
Please get me a taxi.	Per favore, mi trovi un taxi.	pair fahvoaray mee trawvee oon "taxi"
What's the fare to...?	Qual è il prezzo della corsa fino a...?	kwahl ai eel prehttsoa dayllah korsah feenoa ah...?
How far is it to...?	Quanto dista...?	kwahntoa deestah...?
Take me to...	Mi conduca a...	mee koandookah ah
this address	questo indirizzo	kooaystoa eendeereettsoa
the town centre	in centro città	een chayntroa cheettah
the...Hotel	all'albergo...	ahllahlbayrgoa
Turn...at the next corner.	Al prossimo angolo giri...	ahl prossseemoa ahnggoloa jeeree
left/right	a sinistra/a destra	ah seeneestrah/ah dehstrah
Go straight ahead.	Vada sempre diritto.	vahdah sehmpray deereettoa
Please stop here.	Per favore si fermi qui.	pair fahvoaray see fayrmee kooee
I'm in a hurry.	Ho fretta.	oa frayttah
Could you drive more slowly?	Può andare più lentamente?'	pwo ahndarray peeoo lehntahmayntay
Could you help me to carry my bags?	Può aiutarmi a portare le mie borse?	pwo ighootarrmee ah portahray lay meeay borsay

ARRIVAL

Hotel—Other accommodation

Early reservation (and confirmation) is essential in most major tourist centres during the high season. Most towns and arrival points have a tourist information office (*azienda di soggiorno e turismo*—ahdzee**ehn**dah dee sod**joar**noa ay too**rees**moa), and that's the place to go if you're stuck without a room.

It's wise to remember that various surcharges may be added to your hotel bill; the Italian tourist organization, E.N.I.T., publishes an annual directory of all hotels in Italy with details of minimum and maximum prices and facilities.

HOTEL

albergo (ahl**bayr**goa)	The usual word for "hotel" in Italian is *albergo*. Hotels in Italy are classified as *di lusso* (dee **loosss**oa— international luxury class) or first, second, third or fourth class.
appartamento ammobiliato (ahppahrtah**mayn**toa ahmmoabee**leeah**toa)	Furnished flat (apartment). Contact a specialized travel agent if this is the type of arrangement you're looking for.
locanda (lo**kahn**dah)	A country inn.
motel (mo**tehl**)	Increasing in number, improving in service, the Automobile Association of Italy has a list of recommended motels.
pensione (paynsee**oa**nay)	Corresponds to a boarding house; it usually offers *pensione completa*(...koam**play**tah—full board) or *mezza pensione* (**mehd**dzah...—half board). Meals are likely to be from a set menu. *Pensione* are classified first, second or third class.

Note: Especially near railway stations, one often finds *alberghi diurni* (ahl**bayr**gee dee**oor**nee—"daytime hotels"). These have no sleeping accommodation, but provide bathrooms, rest rooms, hairdressers, and other similar services. Most close at midnight.

FOR YOUTH HOSTELS/CAMPING, see page 89

In this section, we're mainly concerned with the smaller and medium-priced hotels and boarding houses. You'll have no language difficulties in the luxury and first-class hotels where most of the staff speak English.

In the next few pages we consider your requirements—step by step—from arrival to departure. You needn't read all of it; just turn to the situation that applies.

Checking in—Reception

My name is...	Mi chiamo...	mee keeearmoa
I've a reservation.	Ho fatto una prenotazione.	oa fahttoa oonah praynoatahtseeoanay
We've reserved two rooms, a single and a double.	Abbiamo prenotato due camere, una singola e una matrimoniale.	ahbbeearmoa praynoatah-toa dooay karmayray oonah seenggoalah ay oonah mahtreemoneeahlay
I wrote to you last month.	Vi ho scritto il mese scorso.	vee oa skreettoa eel maizay skorsoa
Here's the confirmation.	Ecco la conferma.	ehkkoa lah konfehrmah
I'd like a...room...	Vorrei una camera...	vorraiee oonah karmayrah
single	singola	seenggoalah
double	matrimoniale	mahtreemoneeahlay
with twin beds	con due letti	kon dooay lehttee
with a bath	con bagno	kon barñoa
with a shower	con doccia	kon dotchah
with a balcony	con terrazzo	kon tayrrattsoa
with a view	con vista	kon veestah
I'd like a suite.	Vorrei un appartamento.	vorraiee oon ahppahrtah-mayntoa
We'd like a room...	Vorremmo una camera...	vorrehmmoa oonah karmayrah
in the front	sul davanti	sool dahvahntee
at the back	sul retro	sool raitroa
facing the sea	sul mare	sool marray
facing the courtyard	sul cortile	sool korteelay

HOTEL

It must be quiet.	Deve essere tranquilla.	dayvay ehsssayray trahngkooeellah
Is there…?	C'è…?	chai
air conditioning	l'aria condizionata	larreeah kondeetseeonartah
heating	il riscaldamento	eel reeskahldahmayntoa
a radio/television in the room	la radio/il televisore nella stanza	lah rardeeoa/eel taylayveezoaray nayllah stahntsah
laundry service	il servizio di lavanderia	eel sayrveetseeoa dee lahvahndayreeah
room service	il servizio nella stanza	eel sayrveetseeoa nayllah stahntsah
hot water	l'acqua calda	lahkkwah kahldah
running water	l'acqua corrente	lahkkwah korraintay
a private toilet	il gabinetto privato	eel gahbeenayttoa preevahtoa

How much?

What's the price…?	Qual è il prezzo…?	kwahl ai eel prehttsoa
per week	per una settimana	pair oonah saytteemarnah
per night	per una notte	pair oonah nottay
for bed and breakfast	per la camera e la colazione	pair lah karmayrah ay lah koalahtseeoanay
excluding meals	pasti esclusi	parstee ayskloozee
for full board	per la pensione completa	pair lah paynseeoanay koamplaytah
for half board	per mezza pensione	pair mehdzah paynseeoanay

Does that include…?	Il prezzo comprende…?	eel prehttsoa koampraynday
breakfast	la colazione	lah koalahtseeoanay
meals	i pasti	ee parstee
service	il servizio	eel sayrveetseeoa
value-added tax*	l'I.V.A.	leevah
Is there any reduction for children?	C'è una riduzione per i bambini?	chai oonah reedootseeoanay pair ee bahmbeenee
Do you charge for the baby?	Fate pagare per il bambino?	fahtay pahgarray pair eel bahmbeenoa
That's too expensive.	È troppo caro.	ai troppoa karroa
Haven't you anything cheaper?	Non ha nulla di meno caro?	noan ah noollah dee mainoa karroa

---

* Americans note: a type of sales tax.

FOR NUMBERS, see page 176

How long?

We'll be staying…	**Resteremo…**	raystayraymoa
overnight only	**una notte**	oonah nottay
a few days	**qualche giorno**	kwahlkay joarnoa
a week (at least)	**una settimana (come minimo)**	oonah saytteemarnay (koamay meeneemoa)
I don't know yet.	**Non ho ancora deciso.**	noan oa ahngkoarah daycheessoa

Decision

May I see the room?	**Posso vedere la camera?**	posssoa vaydayray lah karmayrah
No, I don't like it.	**No, non mi piace.**	noa noan mee peeahchay
It's too…	**È troppo…**	ai troppoa
cold/hot	**fredda/calda**	frayddah/kahldah
dark/small	**buia/piccola**	booeeah/peekkoalah
noisy	**rumorosa**	roomoaroazah
I asked for a room with a bath.	**Ho chiesto una camera con bagno.**	oa keeeehstoa oonah karmayrah kon barñoa
Do you have anything…?	**Ha qualcosa…?**	ah kwahlkawssah
better/bigger	**migliore/più grande**	meelyoaray/peeoo grahnday
cheaper	**meno caro**	mainoa karroa
quieter	**più tranquillo**	peeoo trahngkooeelloa
higher up	**più in alto**	peeoo een ahltoa
lower down	**più in basso**	peeoo een bahsssoa
Do you have a room with a better view?	**Ha una camera con una vista più bella?**	ah oonah karmayrah kon oonah veestah peeoo baillah
That's fine. I'll take it.	**Va bene, la prendo.**	vah bainay lah prehndoa

Bills

These are usually paid weekly. Most hotels offer a reduction for children under 12.

FOR DAYS OF THE WEEK, see page 181

HOTEL

Tipping

A service charge (15–20 %) is normally included in the bill, but you can ask:

| Is service included ? | È compreso il servizio ? | ai koamprayssoa eel sayrveetseeoa |

Registration

Upon arrival in a hotel or boarding house you'll be asked to fill in a registration form (*una scheda*—**oo**nah **skay**dah). It asks your name, home address, passport number and further destination. It's almost certain to carry an English translation. If it doesn't, ask the desk-clerk (*portiere*– poartee**ay**ray):

| What does this mean ? | Cosa significa questo ? | kawssah seeñeefeekah kooaystoa |

The desk-clerk will ask you for your passport. He may want to keep it for a while. Don't worry. You'll get it back.

Mi può mostrare il passaporto ?	May I see your passport ?
Vuol compilare la scheda, per cortesia ?	Would you mind filling in this registration form ?
Firmi qui, per favore.	Sign here, please.
Quanto tempo si trattiene ?	How long will you be staying ?

| What's my room number? | Qual è il numero della mia stanza ? | kwahl ai eel noomayroa dayllah meeah stahntsah |
| Will you have our bags sent up? | Vuole portare i nostri bagagli in camera ? | vvawlay portarray ee nostree bargahlyee een karmayrah |

FOR TIPPING, see page 1

Service, please

bellboy	**fattorino**	fahttoreenoa
maid	**cameriera (nelle camere)**	kahmayreeayrah
manager	**direttore**	deerayttoaray
room service	**valletto**	vahllayttoa
switchboard operator	**centralinista**	chayntrarleeneestah
waiter	**cameriere**	kahmayreeayray
waitress	**cameriera**	kahmayreeayrah

Call the members of the staff *signore, signorina* or *signora*.
Address the waiter as *cameriere* when calling for service.

General requirements

Please ask the maid to come up.	**Per favore, dica alla cameriera di salire.**	pair fahvoaray deekah ahllah kahmayreeayrah dee sahleeray
Who is it?	**Chi è?**	kee ai
Just a minute.	**Un attimo.**	oon artteemoa
Come in!	**Avanti.**	ahvahntee
Is there a bath on this floor?	**C'è la stanza da bagno a questo piano?**	chai lah stahntsah dah barñoa ah kooaystoa peearnoa
How does this shower work?	**Come funziona questa doccia?**	kawmay foontseeoanah kooaystah dotchah
Where's the plug for the shaver?	**Dov'è la spina per il rasoio?**	doavai lah speenah pair eel rarzoaeeoa
Can we have breakfast in our room?	**Possiamo avere la colazione in camera?**	possseearmoa ahvayray lah koalahtseeoanay een karmayrah
I'd like to leave these in your safe.	**Vorrei depositare questi nella vostra cassaforte.**	vorraiee daypozeetarray kooaystee nayllah vostrah kahsssahfortay
Can you find me a baby-sitter?	**Può trovarmi una baby-sitter?**	pwo trawvahrmee oonah "baby-sitter"

> ### SUONARE PER IL SERVIZIO
> RING FOR SERVICE

HOTEL SERVICE

May I have a/an/some...?	**Posso avere...?**	posssoa ahvayray
ashtray	**un portacenere**	oon portahchaynayray
bath towel	**un asciugamano da bagno**	oon ahshoogarmarnoa dah barñoa
extra blanket	**una coperta in più**	oonah kopehrtah een peeoo
hangers	**degli attaccapanni**	daylyee ahttahkkahparnnee
ice cubes	**dei cubetti di ghiaccio**	daiee koobehttee dee geeahtchoa
extra pillow	**un guanciale in più**	oon gwahncheearlay een peeoo
reading-lamp	**una lampada**	oonah lahmpahdah
soap	**del sapone**	dayl sahpoanay
Where's the...?.	**Dov'è...?**	doavai
barber's	**il barbiere**	eel bahrbeeehray
bathroom	**la stanza da bagno**	lah stahntsah dah barñoa
dining-room	**la sala da pranzo**	lah sarlah dah prahndzoa
hairdresser's	**la parrucchiera**	lah pahrrookkeeayrah
restaurant	**il ristorante**	eel reestorahntay
television room	**la sala della televisione**	lah sarlah dayllah taylay-veezeeoanay
toilet	**il gabinetto**	eel garbeenayttoa

Breakfast

The Italian breakfast consists of coffee, *brioches* (bree**osh**), *focaccia* (foa**kaht**cheeah—crisp buns and flaky pastry) and *marmellata* (mahrmayl**lar**tah—jam). Some hotels can also provide an English or American breakfast.

I'll have a/an/some...	**Desidero...**	dayzeedayroa
bacon and eggs	**uova e pancetta**	wawvah ay pahnchehttah
cereal	**dei fiocchi d'avena**	daiee feeokkee darvaynah
hot/cold	**caldi/freddi**	kahldee/frayddee
eggs	**delle uova**	dayllay wawvah
boiled egg	**uovo alla coque**	wawvoa ahllah kok
soft/medium/hard	**molli/mezza cottura/sode**	mollee/mehddzah kottoorah/soday
fried eggs	**uova fritte**	wawvah freettay
scrambled eggs	**uova strapazzate**	wawvah strahpahttsartay

fruit juice	un succo di frutta	oon sookkoa dee froottah
grapefruit/orange	pompelmo/arancia	pompaylmoa/ahrahn-chah
ham and eggs	prosciutto e uova	proashoottoa ay wawvah
jam	della marmellata	dayllah mahrmayllartah
marmalade	della marmellata d'arance	dayllah mahrmayllartah dahrahnchay
omelet	una frittata	oonah freettartah
pancakes	delle frittelle	dayllay freettehllay
toast	un toast	oon "toast"
yoghurt	uno yogurt	oonoa eeawgoort
May I have some...?	Posso avere un po di...?	posssoa ahvayray oon po dee
hot milk/cold milk	latte caldo/latte freddo	lahttay kahldoa/lahttay frayddoa
cream/sugar	panna/zucchero	pahnnah/tsookkayroa
bread/rolls	pane/panini	parnay/parneenee
butter	burro	boorroa
salt/pepper	sale/pepe	sarlay/paypay
coffee/tea	caffè/tè	kahffai/tai
chocolate	cioccolato	choakkaolartoa
lemon/honey	limone/miele	leemoanay/meeaylay
hot water	acqua calda	ahkkwah kahldah
Could you bring me a...?	Può portarmi...?	pwo portarmee
plate	un piatto	oon peeahttoa
glass/cup	un bicchiere/una tazza	oon beekkeeayray/oonah tahttsah
knife	un coltello	oon koltehlloa
fork	una forchetta	oonah forkehttah
spoon	un cucchiaio	oon kookkeeighoa

Difficulties

The...doesn't work.	...non funziona.	noan foontseeoanah
air-conditioner	il condizionatore d'aria	eel koandeetseeoanahtoaray darreeah
fan	il ventilatore	eel vaynteelahtoaray
heating	il riscaldamento	eel reeskahldahmayntoa
light	la luce	lah loochay
radio	la radio	lah rardeeoa
tap	il rubinetto	eel roobeenayttoa
toilet	il gabinetto	eel gahbeenayttoa
ventilator	la ventilazione	lah vaynteelahtseeoanay

HOTEL SERVICE

FOR EATING OUT, see pages 38–64

The wash-basin is clogged.	Il lavabo è otturato.	eel lahvarboa ai ottoo-rartoa
The window is jammed.	La finestra è incastrata.	lah feenehstrah ai eengkahstrartah
The blind is stuck.	L'imposta è bloccata.	leempoastah ai blokkartah
These aren't my shoes.	Queste non sono le mie scarpe.	kooaystay noan soanoa lay meeay skahrpay
This isn't my laundry.	Questa non è la mia biancheria.	kooaystah noan ai lah meeah beeahngkayreeah
There's no hot water.	Non c'è acqua calda.	noan chai ahkkwah kahldah
I've lost my watch.	Ho perso l'orologio.	oa pairsao loaroaloajoa
I've left my key in my room.	Ho lasciato la chiave nella mia stanza.	oa lahsheeartoa lah keear-vay nayllah meeah stahntsah
The...is broken/ burned out.	...è rotto (rotta)/ bruciata.	...ai rottoa (rottah) broochahtah
bulb	la lampadina	lah lahmpahdeenah
lamp	la lampada	lah lahmpahdah
plug	la spina	lah speenah
shutter	l'imposta	leempoastah
switch	l'interruttore	leentayrroottoaray
venetian blind	la persiana alla veneziana	lah pairseearnah ahllah vaynaytseearnah
window shade	la tendina	lah tayndeenah
Can you get it repaired?	Può ripararlo?	pwo reepahrahrloa

Telephone—Mail—Callers

Can you get me Rome 123-45-67?	Può passarmi Roma 123-45-67?	pwo pahsssahrmee roamah 123-45-67
Did anyone telephone me?	Mi ha telefonato qualcuno?	mee ah taylayfoanartoa kwahlkoonoa
Do you have stamps?	Ha dei francobolli?	ah daiee frahngkoaboallee
Would you please mail this for me?	Può spedirmi questo, per favore?	pwo spaydeermee kooaystoa pair fahvoaray
Are there any messages for me?	Vi sono messaggi per me?	vee soanoa maysssahdjee pair may

FOR POST OFFICE and TELEPHONE, see pages 137–141

Checking out

May I please have my bill?	**Posso avero il conto, per favore?**	pusssoa ahvayray eel koantoa pair fahvoaray
I'm leaving early tomorrow. Please have my bill ready.	**Partirò domani mattina presto. Mi prepari il conto, per favore.**	pahrteeroa doamarnee mahtteenah prehstoa. mee prayparree eel koantoa pair fahvoaray
We'll be checking out around noon.	**Partiremo verso mezzogiorno.**	pahrteeraymoa vehrsoa mehdzoajoarnoa
I must leave at once.	**Devo partire immediatamente.**	dayvoa pahrteeray eemmaydeeahtahmayntay
Is everything included?	**È tutto incluso?**	ai toottoa eengkloozoa
You've made a mistake in this bill, I think.	**Ha fatto un errore nel conto, credo.**	ah fahttoa oon ehrroray nayl koantoa kraydoa
Can you get us a taxi?	**Può chiamarci un taxi?**	pwo keeahmahrchee oon "taxi"
When's the next... to Naples?	**A che ora parte il prossimo...per Napoli?**	ah kay oarah pahrtay eel prossseemoa...pair narpoalee
bus/train/plane	**autobus/treno/ aereo**	owtoaboos/traynoa/ ahairayoa
Would you send someone to bring down our baggage?	**Può mandare qualcuno a portare giù i nostri bagagli?**	pwo mahndarray kwahlkoonoa ah portarray joo ee nostree bahgahlyee
We're in a great hurry.	**Abbiamo molta fretta.**	ahbbeearmoa moaltah frayttah
Here's the forwarding address.	**Ecco il mio prossimo indirizzo.**	ehkkoa eel meeoa prossseemoa eendeereettsoa
You have my home address.	**Avete il mio indirizzo abituale.**	ahvaytay eel meeoa eendeereettsoa ahbeetooarlay
It's been a very enjoyable stay.	**È stato un soggiorno molto piacevole.**	ai startoa oon soadjoarnoa moaltoa peeahchayvoalay
I hope we'll come again sometime.	**Spero che ritorneremo ancora.**	spayroa kay reetornayraymoa ahngkoarah

FOR TAXI, see page 27

HOTEL SERVICE

Eating out

There are various types of places to eat and drink in Italy.
Here are some of them:

Autogrill
(owtoagreel)

Large restaurant on a motorway (turnpike); usually table and cafeteria service available.

Bar

Bar; can be found on virtually every street corner; coffee and drinks served. In most of them you first have to get a ticket from the cashier's. Then you go to the counter and order what you want. Only a few bars have tables and chairs. If you want to be served at a table, the charge for your drinks and food will be somewhat higher. A sign in the window reading *tavola calda* means that simple hot dishes are served.

Caffè
(kahffai)

Coffee shop; generally food isn't served there except for breakfast. If it offers *panini o toasts* you'll be able to get a snack. Coffee shops always serve alcoholic beverages.

Gelateria
(jaylahtayreeah)

Ice-cream parlour; Italian ice-cream is very tasty, rich and creamy, often reminiscent of old-fashioned, homemade ice-cream.

Locanda
(lokahndah)

Simple restaurants serving local dishes.

Osteria
(oastayreeah)

Inn; wine and simple food is served.

Pizzeria
(peettsayreeah)

Pizza parlour; often other dishes are served, too.

Ristorante
(reestoarahntay)

Restaurant; this is the more sophisticated type of eating place. You'll encounter restaurants classified by stars, forks and knives and endorsed by everyone including travel agencies, automobile associations and gastronomic guilds. Bear in mind that any form of classification is relative. Some restaurants are judged according to their

	fancy décor while others—linen and chandeliers aside—are rated merely by the quality of their cooking.
Rosticceria (roasteetchay**ree**ah)	Originally, it was a shop specializing in grilled meats, chicken and fish. But today *rosticcerias* often have tables where you eat grilled food on the premises.
Taverna (tah**vehr**nah)	A more modest type of *trattoria*.
Tea-room	Serves ice-cream and pastries.
Trattoria (trahttoa**ree**ah)	A medium-priced restaurant serving meals and drink. The food is simple but can be surprisingly good if you happen to hit upon the right place.

Meal times

In this section, we're primarily concerned with lunch and dinner. We assume that you've already had breakfast at your hotel or boarding house. See page 34 for a breakfast menu.

Lunch (*il pranzo*—eel **prahn**dzoa) is served from 12.30 to 3 p.m.

Dinner (*la cena*—lah **chay**nah) is usually served later in Italy than at home, seldom beginning before 8 p.m.

The Italians like to linger over a meal so service may seem on the leisurely side. Restaurants close one day per week, often on Monday.

Eating habits

Most restaurants display a menu in the window. Many offer a tourist menu (*menù turistico*), and you'll often find a *piatto del giorno* (pee**aht**toa dayl **joar**noa—dish of the day) too which usually offers you a good meal at a fair price. Words like *del ristorante* or *del cuoco* next to a dish listed on the menu are clues that the dish is a speciality of the restaurant. If the menu mentions *vino incluso,* it means that wine is included in the price of the meal.

The service charge *(servizio)* of usually 12 to 15 per cent, and even the tip *(mancia),* are almost always shown as being included. If the tip isn't included it's entirely up to you. For a snack you may leave some small change, and if you have enjoyed a good meal you may care to leave about 5 per cent on the table for the waiter. Note that you will occasionally also find one or both of the following items added to your bill: *coperto* (cover charge), *supplemento* (surcharge).

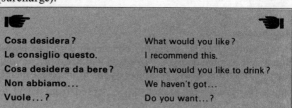

Cosa desidera?	What would you like?
Le consiglio questo.	I recommend this.
Cosa desidera da bere?	What would you like to drink?
Non abbiamo...	We haven't got...
Vuole...?	Do you want...?

Hungry?

I'm hungry/I'm thirsty.	**Ho fame/Ho sete.**	oa farmay/oa saytay
Can you recommend a good restaurant?	**Può consigliarmi un buon ristorante?**	pwo koanseelyahrmee oon bwon reestoarahntay
Are there any inexpensive restaurants around here?	**Vi sono dei ristoranti economici qui vicino?**	vee soanoa daiee reestoarahntee aykoanawmeechee kooee veecheenoa

If you want to be sure of getting a table in a well-known restaurant, it may be better to telephone in advance.

I'd like to reserve a table for 4 people.	**Vorrei riservare un tavolo per 4.**	vorraiee reessayrvarray oon **tar**voaloa pair 4
We'll come at 8.	**Verremo alle 8.**	vayrraymoa ahllay 8

Asking and ordering

Good evening. I'd like a table for 3.	**Buona sera. Vorrei un tavolo per 3.**	bwonah sayrah. vorraiee oon **tar**voaloa pair 3
Could we have a table...?	**Potremmo avere un tavolo...?**	poatraymmca ahvayray oon **tar**voaloa
in the corner	**d'angolo**	dahng**goa**loa
by the window	**vicino alla finestra**	veecheenoa ahllah feenaystrah
outside	**all'aperto**	ahllah**pehr**toa
on the terrace	**sulla terrazza**	soollah tayrrahttsah
Where are the toilets?	**Dove sono i gabinetti?**	doavay soanoa ee gahbee**nay**ttee
May I please have the menu?	**Per favore, mi può dare il menù?**	pair fah**voa**ray mee pwo darray eel maynoo
What's this?	**Cos'è questo?**	kaw**ssai** kooaystoa
Do you have...?	**Avete...?**	avaytay
a set menu	**un menù a prezzo fisso**	oon maynoo ah **preht**tsoa **feess**soa
local dishes	**piatti locali**	pee**aht**tee lo**kar**lee
I'd like...	**Vorrei...**	vorraiee
Is service included?	**È compreso il servizio?**	ai koampray**ssoa** eel sayr**veet**seeoa
Could we have a/an..., please?	**Potremmo avere..., per favore?**	poatraymmoa ahvayray... pair fah**voa**ray
ashtray	**un portacenere**	oon portahchaynayray
another chair	**un'altra sedia**	oonahltrah saideeah
glass	**un bicchiere**	oon beekkeeairay
knife	**un coltello**	oon koaltehlloa
napkin	**un tovagliolo**	oon toavahlyawloa
plate	**un piatto**	oon peeahttoa
serviette	**un tovagliolo**	oon toavahlyawloa
spoon	**un cucchiaio**	oon kookkeeighoa
toothpick	**uno stuzzicadenti**	oonoa stoottseekahdehntee

I'd like a/an/some...	Vorrei...	vorraiee
aperitif	un aperitivo	oon ahpayreeteevoa
appetizer	un antipasto	oon ahnteeparstoa
beer	una birra	oonah beerrah
bread	del pane	dayl parnay
butter	del burro	dayl boorroa
cabbage	dei cavoli	daiee karvoalee
chips (Br.)	delle patatine fritte	dayllay pahtahteenay freettay
cheese	del formaggio	dayl foarmahdjoa
coffee	un caffè	oon kahffai
dessert	un dessert	oon dayssssehrt
eggs	delle uova	dayllay wawvvah
fish	del pesce	dayl payshay
french fries	delle patatine fritte	dayllay pahtahteenay freettay
fruit	della frutta	dayllah froottah
game	della cacciagione	dayllah kahtchahjoanay
ice-cream	un gelato	oon jaylartoa
iced water	dell'acqua ghiacciata	dayllahkkwah geeahtchartah
lemon	un limone	oon leemonay
lettuce	della lattuga	dayllah lahttoogah
meat	della carne	dayllah kahrnay
milk	del latte	dayl lahttay
mineral water	dell'acqua minerale	dayllahkkwah meenayryarlay
mustard	della senape	dayllah saynahpay
(olive) oil	dell'olio (d'oliva)	dayllawlyoa (doleevah)
pepper	del pepe	dayl paypay
potatoes	delle patate	dayllay pahtartay
poultry	del pollo	dayl poalloa
rice	del riso	dayl reessoa
rolls	dei panini	daiee pahneenee
salad	dell'insalata	daylleensahlartah
salt	del sale	dayl sarlay
seafood	dei frutti di mare	daiee froottee dee marray
seasoning	del condimento	dayl koandeemayntoa
soup	una minestra	oonah meenehstrah
starter	un antipasto	oon ahnteeparstoa
sugar	dello zucchero	daylloa tsookkayroa
tea	un tè	oon tay
vegetables	delle verdure	dayllay vehrdooray
vinegar	dell'aceto	dayllahchaytoa
water	dell'acqua	dayllahkkwah
wine	del vino	dayl veenoa

What's on the menu?

Our menu is presented according to courses. Under the headings below you'll find alphabetical lists of dishes that might be offered on an Italian menu with their English equivalent. You can also show the book to the waiter. If you want some fruit, for instance, show him the appropriate list and let *him* point to what's available. Use pages 41 and 42 for ordering in general.

Here, then, is our guide to good eating and drinking. Turn to the section you want.

	page
Appetizers	44
Pizza	45
Soups	45
Pasta	46
Eggs and omelets	47
Fish and seafood	47
Meat	50
Game and fowl	52
Sauces	53
Vegetables	54
Cheese	55
Fruit	55
Dessert	56
Drinks	58
Eating light—Snacks	64

Obviously, you're not going to go through every course on the menu. If you've had enough, say:

Nothing more, thanks. **Nient'altro, grazie.** neeehntahltroa grartseeay

Italian cooking remains essentially regional. Each of the nation's 18 regions has its own specialities. The vicinity of Bologna—Emilia Romagna—is renowned for its culinary art. There are, of course, many well-known dishes that are common to all Italy. But here again the terminology may vary from place to place. (There are at least half a dozen names for octopus or squid!) So in the lists that follow, be prepared for regional variations.

EATING OUT

Appetizers

EATING OUT

I'd like an appetizer.	**Vorrei un antipasto.**	vorraiee oon ahnteeparstoa
acciughe	ahtchoogay	anchovies
affettati misti	ahffayttartee meestee	cold cuts of pork
antipasto misto	ahnteeparstoa meestoa	assorted appetizer
carciofi	kahrchofee	artichoke
caviale	kahveearlay	caviar
culatello	koolahtaylloa	smoked pork
frutti di mare	froottee dee marray	mixed seafood
gamberetti	gahmbayrayttee	shrimps
mortadella	moartahdehllah	Bologna sausage
olive	oleevay	olives
farcite	fahrcheetay	stuffed
nere	nehray	black
verdi	vayrdee	green
ostriche	ostreekay	oysters
prosciutto	proashoottoa	ham
affumicato	ahffoomeekartoa	smoked ham
cotto	kottoa	cooked ham
crudo	kroodoa	cured ham
di cinghiale	dee cheenggeearlay	cured wild boar
salame	sahlarmay	salami
tartufi/trifoli	tahrtoofee / treefoalee	(white) truffles

Appetizer specialities

bagna cauda (barñah kahoodah)	Raw vegetables accompagnied by a hot sauce made from anchovies, garlic, oil, butter and sometimes truffles (Piedmont and Italian-speaking Switzerland)
insalata di mare (eensahlartah dee marray)	prawns and squid with lemon, pickles and olives
mozzarella in carrozza (moattsahrayllah een karrottsah)	a fried open-faced sandwich of mozzarella cheese dipped in egg
soppressata (soappraysssartah)	sausage made from pig's head (southern Italy)
torta pasqualina (toartah pahskwahleenah)	artichoke pie with eggs, mushrooms and Parmesan cheese
zucchini ripieni (tsookkeenee reepeeaynee)	stuffed baby marrows (zucchini)

Pizza

Along with *pasta*, this open pie with its plenitude of different fillings is surely Italy's best known culinary export.

A *pizza* (plural *pizze*) may be covered with tomatoes, ham, anchovies, capers, cheese etc. The cheese is *mozzarella*. It's baked at a very high temperature—and must be eaten hot out of the oven. Since the latter is generally open you can watch your *pizza* sizzling succulently while you wait. It won't burn because it's been lightly brushed with olive oil before being placed on the long, metal spatula over the charcoal embers.

Naples is the great place for *pizza*, and here are the best known variations on the theme:

capricciosa (kahpreet**cho**assah)	The cook's speciality
margherita (mahrgay**ree**tah)	Named after Italy's first queen, the *pizza* ingredients, tomato, cheese and basil, reflect the national colours
napoletana (nahpoalay**tar**nah)	The classic *pizza* with anchovies, ham, capers, tomatoes, cheese and oregano
siciliana (seechee**lyar**nah)	With black olives, capers and cheese

Soups

In Italian, soup goes by various names, as the following list shows. Some of these soups may be main-course fare.

brodetto	braw**dayt**toa	broth with beaten eggs and lemon juice
brodo	**braw**doa	bouillon
di manzo	dee **mahn**dzoa	meat
di pollo	dee **poal**loa	chicken
buridda	boo**reed**dah	spicy fish stew
busecca	boo**zayk**kah	tripe with vegetables and seasoning
cacciucco	kaht**chook**koa	spicy seafood stew (chowder)
minestra asciutta	mee**neh**strah ah**shoot**tah	macaroni or rice

minestrina in brodo con fegatini di pollo	meeneh**stree**nah een **braw**doa kon faygah-**tee**nee dee po**al**loa	noodles and chicken livers
minestrone	meeneh**stroa**nay	a thick vegetable soup sprinkled with parmesan cheese
passato di verdura	pahss**sar**toa dee veh**r**doorah	vegetable soup
zuppa	t**soop**pah	soup
alla cacciatora	**ah**llah kahtchah**toa**rah	meat with mushrooms
alla marinara	**ah**llah mahree**narr**ah	spicy fish stew (chowder)
alla veneta	**ah**llah vay**nay**tah	vegetables with white wine and noodles
di datteri di mare	dee **daht**tayree dee **marr**ay	seafood
di fagioli	dee fah**joa**lee	haricot beans
di frutti di mare	dee **froot**tee dee **marr**ay	seafood
di pesce	dee **pay**shay	spicy fish stew (chowder)
di vongole	dee **vong**goalay	clams and white wine

Pasta

Pasta, the generic name for a wide range of noodles and noodle-related dishes, constitutes the traditional Italian first course. Pasta comes in a bewildering variety of sizes and shapes— ribbons, strings, tubes, shells or stars— known under as many different appellations. It can be served on its own, in broth, stuffed with meat, cheese or vegetables or baked in a pie, and is often accompagnied by a highly flavoured sauce such as those found on page 53.

You'll certainly recognize *cannelloni, maccheroni, ravioli* and *spaghetti,* but some of the names of the dishes on a menu are hard to spot as being pasta. Here are a few favourite pasta dishes you may want to try: *agnoletti, canederli* (a speciality of Trentino-Alto Adige), *cappelletti, fettuccine, lasagne al forno, panzarotti, pappardelle con la lepre* (speciality of Tuscany), *tagliatelle* and *tortellini.*

Rice

Particularly in northern Italy, a rice dish is offered as a first course and often replaces the pasta in a meal. Cooked until very tender together with vegetables, meat, herbs, fish and/or seafood, rice may also be served with a sauce.

risi e bisi	reessee ay beessee	rice with peas and bacon (Venice)
riso in bianco	reessoa een beeahngkoa	boiled rice
risotto	reessottoa	rice casserole
con funghi	kon foonggee	with mushrooms
alla milanese	ahllah meelahnehssay	marrow and white wine

Eggs and omelets

I'd like an omelet.	**Vorrei una frittata.**	vorraiee oonah freettartah
frittata	freettartah	omelet
alla trentina	ahllah traynteenah	artichokes, parsley, basil and marjoram
di carciofi	dee kahrchofee	artichokes
di cipolle	dee cheepoallay	onion
di spinaci	dee speenarchee	spinach.
di zucchini	dee tsookkeenee	dried baby marrow (zucchini)
frittatine piemontesi	freettahteenay peeaymoantehssee	a thin omelet with Fontina cheese and cream

Fish and seafood

Don't miss the opportunity to sample some of the wide variety of fresh fish and seafood in coastal areas. Some inland regions offer special preparations of fish from their rivers, lakes and streams. Fish is most commonly baked or poached until just done, then dressed with a delicate sauce.

I'd like some fish.	**Vorrei del pesce.**	vorraiee dayl payshay
What kind of seafood do you have?	**Che genere di frutti di mare avete?**	kay jehnayray dee froottee dee marray ahvaytay
acciughe	ahtchoogay	anchovies
aguglie	ahgoolyay	garfish
anguilla	ahnggooeellah	eel

FOR OTHER EGG DISHES, see page 34

EATING OUT

aragosta	ahrahgoastah	lobster
aringa	ahreenggah	herring
arselle	ahrsehllay	scallops
baccalà	bahkkahlah	dried salt cod
bianchetti	beeahngkayttee	whitebait
branzino	brahndzeenoa	(sea) bass
calamaretti	kahlahmahrayttee	baby squid
calamari	kahlahmarree	squid
carpa	kahrpah	carp
cozze	koatsay	mussels
dentice	dehnteechay	type of sea bream
eperlano	aypayrlarnoa	smelt
gamberetti	gahmbayrayttee	shrimps
gamberi	gahmbayree	crayfish
granchi	grahngkee	crabs
gronghi	groanggee	conger eel
lamprede	lahmprayday	lampreys
luccio	lootchoa	pike
lumache di mare	loomarkay dee marray	sea snails
merlano	mayrlarnoa	whiting
merluzzo	mayrloottsoa	cod
muggine	moodjeenay	grey mullet
nasello	nahssehlloa	coal-fish
orata	oarartah	type of sea bream
ostriche	ostreekay	oysters
passerino	pahsssayreenoa	plaice
pesce persico	payshay pehrseekoa	perch
pesce spada	payshay spardah	swordfish
pianuzza	peeahnoottsah	plaice
polpo	poalpoa	octopus
razza	rahttsah	ray
ricci	reetchee	sea urchins
rombo	roamboa	turbot
salmone	sahlmoanay	salmon
San Pietro	sahn peeehtroa	John Dory
sardine	sahrdeenay	sardines
scampi	skahmpee	prawns
scorfano	skoarfahnoa	sea-scorpion/sculpin
sgombro	zgoambroa	mackerel
seppia	sayppeeah	cuttlefish
sogliola	sawlyoalah	sole
spigola	speegoalah	sea bass
storione	stoareeoanay	sturgeon
tonno	toannoa	tunny (tuna)
triglie	treelyay	red mullet
trota	trawtah	trout
vongole	vonggoalay	clams

To make sure you get your fish served the way you want it, refer to the following list:

baked	al forno	ahl fornoa
boiled	lesso	laysssoa
(deep) fried	(ben) fritto	(bain) freettoa
grilled	alla griglia	ahllah greelyah
marinated	marinato	mahreenartoa
poached	affogato	ahffoagartoa
smoked	affumicato	ahffoomeekartoa
steamed	cotto a vapore	kottoa ah vahpoaray
stewed	in umido	een oomeedoa

Seafood specialities

anguilla alla veneziana
(ahnggooeellah ahllah vaynaytseearnah)

eel cooked in sauce made from tunny (tuna) and lemon (Venice)

baccalà alla vicentina
(bahkkahlah ahllah veechaynteenah)

cod cooked in milk with onion, garlic, parsley, anchovies and cinnamon (Venice)

fritto misto
(freettoa meestoa)

a fry of various small fish and shellfish

pesci in carpione
(payshee een kahrpeeoanay)

boiled fish, cooked in vinegar, served cold with lemon

pesci al cartoccio
(payshee ahl kahrtotchoa)

baked in a parchment envelope with onions, parsley and herbs

polpi in purgatorio
(poalpee een poorgahtoreeoa)

octopus cooked in oil, with tomatoes, parsley, garlic and peppers (Abruzzi)

seppie con carciofi
(sayppeeay kon kahrchofee)

cuttlefish with artichoke (Latium)

sgombri in umido
(zgoambree een oomeedoa)

stewed mackerel in white wine with green peas

stoccafisso
(stoakkahfeesssoa)

dried cod cooked with tomatoes, olives and artichoke

sogliole alla mugnaia
(sawlyolay ahllah mooñareeah)

sole sautéed in butter, garnished with parsley and lemon

triglie alla livornese
(treelyay ahllah leevoarnayssay)

baked red mullet

EATING OUT

Meat

I'd like some...	Vorrei...	vorraiee
beef	**del manzo**	dayl mahndzoa
lamb	**dell'agnello**	dayllahñehlloa
pork	**del maiale**	dayl migharlay
veal	**del vitello**	dayl veetehlloa

animelle di vitello	ahneemehllay dee veetehlloa	sweetbreads
arrosto di manzo	ahrroastoa dee mahndzoa	roast beef
bistecca	beestaykkah	steak
di filetto	dee feelehttoa	rib steak
braciola	brahchoalah	chop
costola	kostoalah	rib
costoletta	koastoalayttah	cutlet
cervello	chayrvehlloa	brains
fegato	faygahtoa	liver
filetto	feelayttoa	fillet
lingua	leenggwah	tongue
lombata/lombo	loambartah / loamboa	loin
midollo	meedoalloa	marrow
montone	moantoanay	mutton
pancetta affumicata	pahnchehttah ahffoomeekartah	bacon
polpette	poalpayttay	meatballs
porchetta	poarkayttah	sucking pig
prosciutto	proashoottoa	ham
rognoni	roañoanee	kidneys
salumi	sahloomee	assorted pork products
salsicce	sahlseetchay	sausages
scaloppina	skahloappoenah	scallop
spalla	spahllah	shoulder
trippe	treeppay	tripe
zampa	tsahmpah	pig's trotter (feet)

Italian meat dishes

Meat is virtually always dressed with some sort of creamy sauce or gravy—sometimes prepared at your table.

abbacchio (ahbbahkkeeoa)	roast lamb, often served in a casserole with anchovies (Latium)
bistecca alla fiorentina (beestaykkah ahllah feeoaraynteenah)	a grilled steak flavoured with pepper, lemon juice and parsley (Tuscany)

cima alla genovese (**cheemah** ahllah jaynoavayssay)	rolled veal stuffed with eggs, sausage and mushrooms (Liguria)
corda (**kor**dah)	lamb tripe roasted or in tomato sauce with green peas (Sardinia)
costata al prosciutto (koastartah ahl proashoottoa)	a chop filled with ham, cheese and truffles; breaded and fried until golden brown (Emilia-Romagna)
costoletta alla milanese (koastoalayttah ahllah meelah-nayssay)	breaded veal cutlet, flavoured with cheese (Lombardy)
farsumagru palermitano (fahrsoomargroo pahlayrmee-tarnoa)	braised meat with chopped hard-boiled eggs (Sicily)
fegato alla veneziana (faygahtoa ahllah vaynaytseearnah)	thin slices of calf's liver fried with onions (Venice)
gulash (**goo**lash)	chunks of beef stewed in paprika sauce
involtini (eenvoalteenee)	chicken-liver balls cooked in beef stock (Emilia-Romagna)
ossi buchi (**oss**see **boo**kee)	veal knuckle and rice braised and served in a highly flavoured sauce (Lombardy)
saltimbocca alla romana (sahlteemboakkah ahllah roamarnah)	escalope of veal braised in marsala wine with ham and sage (Latium)
scaloppina alla Val d'Aosta (skahloappeenah ahllah vahl dahostah)	veal scallop filled with cheese and ham
trippe alla fiorentina (**treep**pay ahllah feeooraynteenah)	tripe and beef braised in a tomato sauce, served with cheese (Tuscany)

How do you like your meat ?

baked	al forno	ahl fornoa
barbecued	alla graticola	ahllah grahteekoalah
boiled	lesso	laysssoa
braised	brasato	brahssartoa
broiled	allo spiedo	ahlloa speeehdoa
en casserole	in casseruola	een kasssayrwoolah
fried	fritto	fteettoa
grilled	ai ferri	ahee fehrree
roasted	arrostito	ahrroasteetoa
stewed	in umido	een oomeedoa
stuffed	farcito	fahrcheetoa
underdone (rare)	al sangue	ahl sahnggooay
medium	a puntino	ah poonteenoa
well-done	ben cotto	bain kottoa

Game and fowl

Many small fowl not regarded as game in America or Britain are served as first or main courses in Italy. They're usually grilled or roasted. Among small fowl considered fair game for the gourmet palate are lark, plover, thrush and ortolan.

I'd like some game.	Vorrei della cacciagione.	vorraiee dayllah kahtchahjoanay
What poultry dishes do you serve ?	Che piatti di pollame servite ?	kay peeahttee dee poallarmay sayrveetay

allodola	ahllodoalah	lark
anatroccolo	ahnahtrokkoaloa	duckling
anitra	arneetrah	duck
beccaccia	baykkahtchah	woodcock
beccaccino	baykkahtcheenoa	snipe
camoscio	kahmoshoa	chamois
cappone	kahppoanay	capon
capretto	kahprayttoa	kid goat
capriolo	kahpreeoloa	roebuck
cervo	chehrvoa	deer
cinghiale	cheenggeearlay	wild boar
coniglio	koaneelyoa	rabbit
fagiano	fahjarnoa	pheasant
faraona	fahrahoanah	guinea fowl

gallina	gahlleenah	stewing fowl
gallo cedrone	gahlloa chehdroanay	grouse
lepre	laipray	hare
oca	okah	goose
ortolano	oartoalarnoa	ortolan
pernice	payrneechay	partridge
piccione	peetchoanay	pigeon
piviere	peeveeehray	plover
pollo	poalloa	chicken
pollo novello	poalloa noavehlloa	spring chicken
porcellino da latte	poarchaylleenoa dah lahttay	sucking pig
quaglia	kwahlyah	quail
selvaggina	saylvahdjeenah	venison
tacchino	tahkkeenoa	turkey
tordo	toardoa	thrush

Game and fowl dishes

capretto ripieno al forno
(kahprayttoa reepeeaynoa ahl fornoa)
stuffed kid, oven-roasted (Apulia, Calabria)

palombacce allo spiedo
(pahloambahtchay ahlloa speeehdoa)
wood pigeon, spit-roasted (Umbria)

polenta e uccelli
(poalehntah ay ootchehllee)
various small birds roasted on a spit and served with a mush made from maize flour (cornmeal mush) (Lombardy)

polenta e coniglio
(poalehntah ay koaneelyoa)
rabbit stew served with polenta (see immediately above) (Venice)

Some common sauces and preparations

pesto alla genovese
(paystoa ahllah jaynoavayssay)
olive oil, basil, cheese, garlic and pine nuts

pommarola alla napoletana
(poammahrolah ahllah napoalaytarnah)
tomatoes

ragù alla bolognese
(rahgoo ahllah boaloañayssay)
minced beef, onions, tomatoes, oil and herbs

salsa alla milanese
(sahlsah ahllah meelahnayssay)
onions, tomatoes, bacon, butter and olive oil

EATING OUT

Vegetables

barbabietole	bahrbahbeeehtoalay	beetroot
carciofi	kahrchofee	artichoke
carote	kahrawtay	carrots
cavolfiore	kahvoalfeeoaray	cauliflower
cavoli	karvoalee	cabbage
cavolini di Bruxelles	kahvoaleenee dee broossayl	brussels sprouts
ceci	chaychee	chick-peas
cetrioli	chaytreeolee	cucumbers
cetriolini	chaytreeoaleenee	gherkins
cicoria	cheekoreeah	endive (U.S. chicory)
cipolle	cheepollay	onions
fagioli	fahjoalee	beans
fagiolini	fahjoaleenee	green beans
fave	farvay	broad beans
finocchi	feenokkee	fennel
funghi	foonggee	mushrooms
indivia	eendeeveeah	chicory (U.S. endive)
insalata	eensahlartah	green salad
lattuga	lahttoogah	lettuce
lenticchie	laynteekkeeay	lentils
mais dolce	maheess doalchay	maize (corn)
melanzane	maylahntsarnay	eggplant
peperoni	paypayroanee	peppers, pimentos
piselli	peessehllee	peas
pomidoro	poameedawroa	tomatoes
porcini	poarcheenee	boletus mushrooms
porri	porree	leaks
primizia	preemeetseeah	spring (adj.)
rape	rarpay	turnips
ravanelli	rahvahnehllee	radishes
riso	reessoa	rice
sedano	sehdahnoa	celery
spinaci	speenarchee	spinach
tartufi bianchi/neri	tahrtoofee beeahngkee/nayree	truffles white/black
topinamburo	toapeenahmbooroa	Jerusalem artichoke
verdura mista	vehrdoorah meestah	mixed vegetables
verza	vehrdzah	green cabbage
zucca	tsookkah	kind of pumpkin (squash)
zucchini	tsookkeenee	vegetable marrow (zucchini)

Cheese

Italy produces a great variety of cheeses, many of them little known outside the locality in which they're made. Cheese is a separate course in many Italian meals, preceding the dessert.

mild cheese	*bel paese, caciocavallo, fontina, mascarpone, mozzarella, parmigiano-reggiano* (which we call parmesan), *provatura, ragusano*	
sharp cheese	*asiago, gorgonzola* (resembles Danish and French blue), *provolone*	
other varieties	*asiago* (sometimes made of ewe's milk), *caciocavallo* (sometimes made of mare's milk), *mozzarella* (still produced with buffalo milk south of Naples), *pecorino* (any of a variety of tangy ewe's milk cheeses), *ricotta* (often made from ewe's milk)	

Fruit

Fruit is generally served after the cheese.

Do you have fresh fruit?	**Avete della frutta fresca?**	ahvaytay dayllah froottah frayskah
I'd like a fresh fruit cocktail.	**Vorrei una scelta di frutta fresca.**	vorraiee oonah shayltah dee froottah frayskah

albicocca	ahlbeekokkah	apricot
ananas	ahnahnahss	pineapple
anguria	ahnggooreeah	watermelon
arancia	ahrahnchah	orange
cachi	karkee	persimmon
castagne	kahstarñay	chestnuts
cedro	chaydroa	lime
ciliege	cheeleeayjay	cherries
cocomero	koakoamayroa	watermelon
fichi	feekee	figs
fragole	frargoalay	strawberries
lamponi	lahmpoanee	raspberries
limone	leemoanay	lemon
mandarini	mahndahreenee	tangerines
mandorle	mahndoarlay	almonds
mela	maylah	apple
mirtilli	meerteellee	blueberries
more	moray	mulberries

EATING OUT

nocciole	noatcholay	hazelnuts
noci	noachee	walnuts
pera	payrah	pear
pesca	pehskah	peach
pompelmo	poampaylmoa	grapefruit
prugna	prooñah	plum
prugna secca	prooñah saykkah	prune
ribes	reebayss	red currants
uva	oovah	grapes

Dessert

As you've probably realized by now, Italian food is filling and you may not feel like a heavy dessert. The Italians feel the same. Few Italian restaurants serve pie or puddings of the substantial sort that we're used to at home. As an alternative, try some of the delicious ice-cream (*gelato*—jay**lar**toa) for which Italy is renowned. A *granita* (grah**nee**tah) makes a refreshing close to a meal. This is made by pouring syrup, juice or coffee over a glass of chipped ice.

I'd like a dessert, please.	**Vorrei un dessert, per favore.**	vorraiee oon daysssehr pair fahvoaray
Something light, please.	**Qualcosa di leggero, per favore.**	kwahlkawssah dee laydjairoa pair fahvoaray
Just a small portion.	**Solo una piccola porzione.**	soaloa oonah peekkoalah portseeoanay
Nothing more, thanks.	**Nient'altro, grazie.**	neeehntahltroa grartseeay

If you aren't sure what to order, ask the waiter:

What do you have for dessert?	**Che dessert avete?**	kay daysssehr ahvaytay
What do you recommend?	**Cosa consiglia?**	kawssah koanseelyah
budino	boodeenoa	pudding
cassata gelata	kahsssartah jaylartah	ice-cream with candied fruit (U.S. spumoni)
cassata siciliana	kahsssartah seecheelyannah	sponge cake garnished with sweet cream cheese, chocolate and candied fruit

crema	kraimah	custard
dolce	doalchay	cake
gelato	jaylartoa	ice-cream
all'amarena	ahllahmahraynah	wild-cherry
alla fragola	ahllah frargoalah	strawberry
al limone	ahl leemoanay	lemon
alla vaniglia	ahllah vahneelyah	vanilla
panforte di Siena	pahnfortay dee seeehnah	cake with candied fruit, cloves and pimento
panicielli d'uva passula	pahneechayllee doovah pahsssoolah	raisins wrapped in lemon leaves

That's the end of our Italian menu. For wine and other drinks, see the next pages. But after the feast comes…

The bill (check)

I'd like to pay.	Vorrei pagare.	vorraiee pahgarray
We'd like to pay separately.	Vorremmo pagare separatamente.	vorrehmmoa pahgarray saypahrahtahmayntay
You've made a mistake in this bill, I think.	Penso che abbiate fatto un errore nel conto.	pehnsoa kay ahbbeeartay fahttoa oon ayrroaray nayl koantoa
Is service included?	È compreso il servizio?	ai koamprayssoa eel sayrveetseeoa
Is everything included?	È tutto compreso?	ai toottoa koamprayssoa
Do you accept traveller's cheques?	Accettate i traveller's cheques?	ahtchayttartay ee "traveller's cheques"
Thank you, this is for you.	Grazie, questo è per lei.	grartseeay kooaystoa ai pair lehee
Keep the change.	Tenga il resto.	taynggah eel rehstoa
That was a very good meal.	È stato un pasto molto buono.	ai startoa oon parstoa moaltoa bwonoa
We enjoyed it, thank you.	Ci è piaciuto grazie.	chee ai peeahchootoa grartseeay

EATING OUT

SERVIZIO COMPRESO
SERVICE INCLUDED

FOR TIPPING, see page 1

Complaints

But perhaps you'll have something to complain about:

That's not what I ordered. I asked for...	**Non è ciò che avevo ordinato. Ho chiesto...**	noan ai cho kay ahvayvoa oardeenartoa. oa keeehstoa
May I change this?	**Posso cambiare questo?**	posssoa kahmbeearray kooaystoa
The meat is...	**La carne è...**	lah kahrnay ai
overdone	**troppo cotta**	troppoa kottah
underdone	**poco cotta**	pokoa kottah
too rare	**troppo al sangue**	troppoa ahl sahnggooay
too tough	**troppo dura**	troppoa doorah
This is too...	**Questo è troppo...**	kooaystoa ai troppoa
bitter / salty	**amaro / salato**	ahmarroa / sahlartoa
sweet	**dolce**	doalchay
The food is cold.	**Il cibo è freddo.**	eel cheeboa ai frayddoa
This isn't fresh.	**Questo non è fresco.**	kooaystoa noan ai frayskoa
What's taking you so long?	**Perchè avete impiegato tanto tempo?**	pehrkai ahvaytay eempeeaygartoa tahntoa tehmpoa
Where are our drinks?	**Dove sono le nostre bevande?**	doavay soanoa lay nostray bayvahnday
This isn't clean.	**Questo non è pulito.**	kooaystoa noan ai pooleetoa
Would you ask the head waiter to come over?	**Vuole chiedere al capo cameriere di venire qui?**	vvwolay keeaydayray ahl karpoa kahmayreeehray dee vayneeray kooee

Drinks
Aperitifs

The average Italian is just as fond of his favourite *aperitivo* (ahpehreeteevoa) as we are of our cocktail or highball. Often bittersweet, some aperitifs have a wine and brandy base with herbs and bitters while others may have a vegetable base. Here are some aperitifs you may want to try:

Americano (ahmayreekarnoa)	despite its name, the most popular Italian aperitif; a vermouth to which bitters, brandy and lemon peel are added

Aperol (ahpay**roal**)	a non-alcoholic bitters
Campari (kahm**pah**ree)	reddish-brown bitters, flavoured with orange peel and herbs, it has a quinine taste
Cynar... (**chee**narr)	produced from artichoke
Martini (mahr**tee**nee)	a brand-name vermouth not to be confused with a martini cocktail
I'd like a Cynar...	**Vorrei un Cynar ...** vorr**ai**ee oon **chee**narr
neat (straight)	**liscio** **lee**shoa
on the rocks	**con ghiaccio** koan gee**ah**tchoa
with (seltzer) water	**con acqua (di seltz)** koan **ah**kkwah (dee **seh**ltz)

Wine

Italy produces nearly 2 thousand million gallons of wine annually and is thus the world's most important wine-producing country in terms of quantity. Vineyards are found all over the Italian peninsula and islands.

Some restaurants list their wines in a corner of the menu while others have them marked up on the wall. As much of the nation's wine doesn't travel well, don't expect a *trattoria* to offer more than a few types of wine. Most of the wine must be drunk young so don't look too hard for vintage labels. Wine—even red—is always served chilled in Italy.

Some of the country's most reputed wines (like *Barbaresco* and *Barolo*) comes from the Piedmont in northwestern Italy. But most other regions have noted wine, too. This is your opportunity to sample local wine, some of which is of surprisingly good quality.

Chianti is doubtless Italy's best-known wine outside of its borders. The best of it is produced between Florence and Siena. The term *Chianti classico* on the label indicates that the production of this wine has been carefully supervised. A *Chianti* of superior quality carries the term *riserva* on the label.

If you need help in choosing a wine, don't hesitate to ask the waiter. He'll often suggest a bottle of local renown.

Italians drink red wine with almost everything. But white wine is reserved for fish and seafood. However, if you're around the Lake of Garda, it's traditional to drink the light red *Bardolino* or *Valpolicella* with lake trout. A good rosé goes well with almost anything. The chart on the following page will help you to choose your wine if you want to do some serious wine-tasting.

I'd like...of...	Vorrei...di...	vorraiee...dee
a carafe	una caraffa	oonah kahrahffah
a bottle	una bottiglia	oonah botteelyah
half a bottle	mezza bottiglia	mehdzah botteelyah
a glass	un bicchiere	oon beekkeeairay
a litre	un litro	oon leetroa
I want a bottle of white / red wine.	Vorrei una bottiglia di vino bianco / rosso.	vorraiee oonah botteelyah dee veenoa beeahngkoa / roasssoa

EATING OUT

dry	secco	sehkkoa
full-bodied	pieno	peeaynoa
light	leggero	laydjairoa
red	rosso	roasssoa
rosé	rosatello	rawzahtehlloa
sparkling	spumante	spoomahntay
sweet	dolce	doalchay
white	bianco	beeahngkoa

If you have enjoyed the wine, you may want to say:

Please bring me another...	Per favore, mi porti...	pair fahvoaray mee portee
glass	un altro bicchiere	oon ahltroa beekkeeairay
carafe	un'altra caraffa	oonahltrah kahrahffah
bottle	un'altra bottiglia	oonahltrah botteelyah
Where does this wine come from ?	Da dove viene questo vino ?	dah doavay veeaynay kooaystoa veenoa

Type of wine	Examples	Accompanies
sweet white wine	*Orvieto* from Umbria (the export variety is usually dry), *Aleatico* and *Vino Santo* from Tuscany and the famed *Marsala* from Sicily	desserts, especially custard, pudding, cake
dry white wine	*Frascati* from Latium or *Verdicchio dei Castelli di Jesi* from the Adriatic Marches; local white wine generally falls into this category	fish, seafood, cold or boiled meat, fowl (the unconventional Romans enjoy drinking *Frascati* with a heavy meal)
rosé	*Lagrein* from Trentino-Alto Adige	goes with almost anything but especially cold dishes, eggs, pork and lamb
light-bodied red wine	*Bardolino* and *Valpolicella* from the Lake of Garda; local red wine, including Italian-Swiss *Merlot,* usually fits this category	roast chicken, turkey, veal, lamb, steaks, ham, liver, quail, pheasant, soft-textured cheeses, stews and pasta
full-bodied red wine	*Barolo* and *Barbaresco* from Piedmont	duck, goose, kidneys, most game, tangy cheese like *gorgonzola*—in short, any strong-flavoured dishes
sparkling white wine	*Asti spumante* (Italians like to refer to it as champagne but it's slightly sweet)	goes nicely with dessert and pastry; if it's dry, you might try *spumante* as an aperitif or with shellfish, nuts or dried fruit

EATING OUT

Other alcoholic drinks

Coffee shops and bars usually have a good stock of foreign and domestic beer, wine and liquor—even some of your favourite brands. Don't bother asking for any fancy cocktails or highballs except in the more sophisticated establishments or where signs are displayed saying *American bar*. Though not particularly noted for its beer, Italy does produce a number of local brews, especially in the North, which you might like to sample.

aperitif	un aperitivo	oon ahpayreeteevoa
beer	una birra	oonah beerrah
Bourbon	un Bourbon	oon "bourbon"
brandy	un brandy	oon "brandy"
cider	del sidro	dayl seedroa
cognac	un cognac	oon koañahk
cordial (Am.)	un liquore	oon leekwoaray
gin	un gin	oon "gin"
gin-fizz	un gin-fizz	oon "gin-fizz"
gin and tonic	un gin e tonico	oon "gin" ay toneekoa
liqueur	un liquore	oon leekwoaray
port	un porto	oon portoa
rum	un rum	oon room
Scotch	uno Scotch	oonoa "scotch"
sherry	uno sherry	oonoa "sherry"
vermouth	un vermouth	oon vehrmoot
vodka	della vodka	dayllah vodkah
whisky	un whisky	oon "whisky"
whisky and soda	whisky e soda	"whisky" ay sodah

glass	un bicchiere	oon beekkeeairay
bottle	una bottiglia	oonah botteelyah
double (a double shot)	doppio	doappeeoa
neat (straight)	liscio	leeshoa
on the rocks	con ghiaccio	kon geeahtchoa

You'll certainly want to take the occasion to sip an after-dinner drink. If you'd like something which approaches French cognac try *Vecchia Romagna*. If you feel a digestive is called for, a glass of *Fernet-Branca* should fit the bill.

EATING OUT

I'd like to try a glass of..., please.	**Vorrei assaggiare un bicchiere di..., per favore.**	vorraiee ahsssahdjarray oon beekkeeairay dee... pair fahvoaray
Are there any local specialities?	**Avete specialità locali?**	ahvaytay spaychahleetah loakarlee
Please bring me a... of...	**Per favore, mi porti un...di...**	pair fahvoaray mee portee oon...dee

> **CIN-CIN!**
> (cheen cheen)
> **CHEERS!**

Soft drinks, coffee, tea

The Italian *caffè espresso* has a rich aroma and is excellent everywhere. Served in demi-tasses, it's stronger than what we're used to at home. However, if you'd like to try a more concentrated cup of espresso coffee, ask for a *ristretto* (reestrayttoa). As against this, a *caffè lungo* (kahffay loonggoa) is a slightly weaker cup of espresso coffee.

For breakfast don't miss the opportunity to drink a *cappuccino* (kahppootcheenoa), a delicious mixture of coffee and hot milk, dusted with cocoa. In summer, iced tea and coffee are popular.

I'd like a/an...	**Vorrei...**	vorraiee
chocolate	**un cioccolato**	oon choakkoalartoa
coffee	**un caffè**	oon kahffay
cup of coffee	**una tazza di caffè**	oonah tahttsah dee kahffay
coffee with cream	**un caffè con panna**	oon kahffay kon pahnnah
espresso coffee	**un caffè espresso**	oon kahffay aysprehsssoa
iced coffee	**un caffè freddo**	oon kahffay frayddoa
fruit juice	**un succo di frutta**	oon sookkoa dee froottah
grapefruit	**di pompelmo**	dee poampaylmoa
lemon	**di limone**	dee leemoanay
orange	**d'arancia**	dahrahnchah
pineapple	**d'ananas**	dahnahnahss
tomato	**di pomodoro**	dee poamoadawroa
lemonade	**una limonata**	oonah leemoanartah

EATING OUT

milk	del latte	dayl lahttay
milkshake	un frullato di latte	oon froollartoa dee lahttay
mineral water	dell'acqua minerale	dayllahkkwah meenayrarlay
orangeade	un'aranciata	oonahrahnchartah
soda water	dell'acqua di seltz	dayllahkkwah dee sehlts
squash (fruit drink)	una spremuta	oonah spraymootah
tea	un tè	oon tay
with milk / lemon	con latte / limone	kon lahttay/leemoanay
iced tea	un tè freddo	oon tay frayddoa
tonic water	dell'acqua tonica	dayllahkkwah toneekah

Eating light—Snacks

I'll have one of those, please.	Per favore, vorrei uno di questi.	pair fahvoaray vorraiee oonoa dee kooaystee
Give me two of these and one of those.	Mi dia due di questi e uno di quelli.	mee deeah dooay dee kooaystee ay oonoa dee kooayllee
to the left / right	a sinistra / a destra	ah seeneestrah/ah dehstrah
above / below	sopra / sotto	soaprah/soattoa
Please give me a / an / some...	Per favore, mi dia...	pair fahvoaray mee deeah
biscuits (Br.)	dei biscotti	daiee beeskottee
bread	del pane	dayl parnay
butter	del burro	dayl boorroa
cake	della torta	dayllah toartah
candy	un dolce	oon doalcheh
(bar of) chocolate	(una stecca di) cioccolata	(oonah staykkah dee) choakkoalartah
cookies	dei biscotti	daiee beeskottee
hamburger	un hamburger	oon ahmboorgayr
hot-dog	un hot dog	oon "hot dog"
ice-cream	un gelato	oon jaylartoa
pastry	dei dolci	daiee doalchee
pie	un pasticcio	oon pahsteetchoa
roll	un panino	oon pahneenoa
salad	un'insalata	ooneensahlartah
sandwich	un sandwich	oon "sandwich"
sweets	dei dolciumi	daiee doalchoomee
toast	un toast	oon "toast"
waffles	delle cialde	dayllay chahlday
How much is that?	Quant'è?	kwahntai

Travelling around

Plane

Very brief—because at any airline office or airport you're sure to find someone who speaks English. But here are a few useful expressions you may want to know:

Do you speak English?	**Parla inglese?**	pahrlah eengglayssay
Is there a flight to Naples?	**C'è un volo per Napoli?**	chai oon **vo**aloa pair narpoalee
Is it a nonstop flight?	**È un volo diretto?**	ai oon **vo**aloa deerayttoa
When's the next plane to Palermo?	**A che ora parte il prossimo aereo per Palermo?**	ah kay oarah **pahr**tay eel **pross**seemoa ahairayoa pair pah**leh**rmoa
Do I have to change planes?	**Devo cambiare aereo?**	dayvoa kahmbee**ar**ray ahairayoa
Can I make a connection to Venice?	**Posso prendere una coincidenza per Venezia?**	**poss**soa **prehn**dayray oonah koeencheede**hn**tsah pair vaynaytseeah
I'd like a ticket to Milan.	**Vorrei un biglietto per Milano.**	vorraiee oon beel**yay**ttoa pair meelarnoa
What's the fare to Torino?	**Quanto costa il biglietto per Torino?**	**kwahn**toa kostah eel beel**yay**ttoa pair toareenoa
single (one-way) return (roundtrip)	**andata** **andata e ritorno**	ahn**dar**tah ahn**dar**tah ay reetornoa
What time does the plane take off?	**A che ora decolla l'aereo?**	ah kay oarah day**koll**ah lahairayoa
What time do I have to check in?	**Quanto tempo ho prima del controllo?**	**kwahn**toa **tehm**poa oa preemah dayl koantrolloa
What's the flight number?	**Qual è il numero del volo?**	kwahl ai eel **noo**mayroa dayl **vo**aloa
What time do we arrive?	**A che ora arriveremo?**	ah kay oarah ahrreevay**ray**moa

ARRIVO	**PARTENZA**
ARRIVAL	DEPARTURE

TRAVELLING AROUND

Trains

If you are worried about railway tickets or time-tables, go to a travel agency where they speak English or see the *portiere* (poarteeayray) of your hotel.

Train travel in Italy is usually fast on the main lines. The trains (diesel and electric) run on time, although there may be delays during the tourist season. First-class coaches are comfortable: second-class, adequate.

Types of trains

TEE (teh-eh-eh)	A luxury, international service with first class only; additional fare and reservation required
Rapido (R.) (rarpeedoa)	Long-distance express luxury coaches; additional fare required
Direttissimo (D. D.) (deerehtteessseemoa)	Long-distance train, stopping at main stations
Diretto (D.) (deerehttoa)	Local train, stopping at the main stations
Accelerato (A.) (ahtchaylayrartoa)	Small local train, stopping at all stations
Locale (L.) (loakarlay)	Same as an *accelerato*

Here are some more useful terms which you may need.

Littorina (leettoareenah)	Small diesel used on short runs
Vagone letto (vahgonay lehttoa)	Sleeping-car with individual compartments and washing facilities
Carrozza cuccette (kahrrottsah kootchehttay)	A berth with blankets and pillows
Carrozza ristorante (kahrrottsah reestorahntay)	Dining-car
Bagagliaio (bahgahlyeeareeoa)	Guard's van (baggage car): normally only registered luggage permitted

TRAVELLING AROUND

To the railway station

Where's the railway station?	Dove si trova la stazione ferroviaria?	doavay see trawvah lah stahtseeoanay fehrrovee-arreeah
Taxi, please!	Taxi, per favore!	"taxi" pair fahvoaray
Take me to the railway station.	Mi porti alla stazione ferroviaria.	mee portee ahllah staht-seeoanay fehrroveearreeah
What's the fare?	Quant'è?	kwahntai

Where's the...?

Where is/are the...?	Dove si trova...?	doavay see trawvah
barber's shop	il barbiere	eel barbeeairay
booking office	l'ufficio prenotazioni	looffeecheeoa praynoatahtseeoanee
buffet	il buffet	eel booffay
currency-exchange office	l'ufficio cambio	looffeecheeoa kahmbeeoa
information office	l'ufficio informazioni	looffeecheeoa eenfoarmahtseeoanee
left-luggage office (baggage check)	il deposito bagagli	eel daypozeetoa bahgahlyee
lost-property (lost-and-found) office	l'ufficio oggetti smarriti	looffeecheeoa odjehttee smahrreetee
luggage lockers	la custodia automatica dei bagagli	lah koostodeeah owtoa-marteekah daiee bahgahlyee
news-stand	l'edicola	laydeekoalah
platform 7	il binario 7	eel beenarreeoa 7
reservations office	l'ufficio prenotazioni	looffeecheeoa praynoatahtseeoanee
restaurant	il ristorante	eel reestorahntay
snack bar	lo "snack bar"	loa "snack bar"
ticket office	la biglietteria	lah beelyayttayreeah
waiting-room	la sala d'aspetto	lah sarlah dahspehtto
Where are the toilets?	Dove sono i gabinetti?	doavay soanoa ee gahbeenayttee

---

INFORMAZIONI TURISTICHE TOURIST INFORMATION
UFFICIO CAMBIO CURRENCY EXCHANGE

FOR TAXI, see page 27

TRAVELLING AROUND

Inquiries

When is the...train to Rome?	**Quando parte... treno per Roma?**	kwahndoa pahrtay... traynoa pair roamah
first/last next	**il primo/l'ultimo il prossimo**	eel preemoa/loolteemoa eel prossseemoa
What time does the train for Milan leave?	**A che ora parte il treno per Milano?**	ah kay oarah pahrtay eel traynoa pair meelarnoa
What's the fare to Ancona?	**Quanto costa il biglietto per Ancona?**	kwahntoa kostah eel beelyeeehttoa pair ahngkoanah
Is it a through train?	**È un treno diretto?**	ai oon traynoa deerehttoa
Will the train leave on time?	**Partirà in orario il treno?**	pahrteerah een oararreeoo eel traynoa
What time does the train arrive at Florence?	**A che ora arriverà a Firenze il treno?**	ah kay oarah ahrreevayrah ah feerehntsay eel traynoa
Is there a dining-car on the train?	**C'è una carrozza ristorante sul treno?**	chai oonah kahrrottsah reestorahntay sool traynoa
Is there a sleeping-car on the train?	**C'è un vagone letto sul treno?**	chai oon vahgonay lehttoa sool traynoa
Does the train stop at Lugano?	**Il treno si fermerà a Lugano?**	eel traynoa see fayrmayrah ah loogarnoa
What platform does the train for Verona leave from?	**Da che binario parte il treno per Verona?**	dah kay beenarreeoa pahrtay eel traynoa pair vayroanah
What platform does the train from Bari arrive at?	**A che binario arriva il treno proveniente da Bari?**	ah kay beenarreeoa ahrreevah eel traynoa provayneeehntay dah barree
I'd like to buy a time-table.	**Vorrei comperare un orario ferroviario.**	vorraie koampayrarray oon oararreeoa fehrroveearreeoa

ENTRATA	ENTRANCE
USCITA	EXIT
AI BINARI	TO THE PLATFORMS

È un treno diretto.	It's a through train.
Deve cambiare a...	You have to change at...
Cambi a...e prenda un treno locale.	Change at...and get a local train.
Il binario 7 è...	Platform 7 is...
laggiù/su dalle scale a sinistra/a destra	over there/upstairs on the left/on the right
C'è un treno per... alle...	There's a train to... at...
Il suo treno partirà dal binario...	Your train will leave from platform...
Ci sarà un ritardo di... minuti.	There'll be a delay of... minutes.

Tickets

I want a ticket to Rome.	Desidero un biglietto per Roma.	dayzeedayroa oon beelyayttoa pair roamah
single (one-way)	andata	ahndartah
return (roundtrip)	andata e ritorno	ahndartah ay reetorrnoa
first class	prima classe	preemah klahsssay
Isn't it half price for the child?	Non si paga metà prezzo per il bambino?	noan see pargah maytah prehttsoa pair eel bahmbeenoa
He's/She's 13*.	Ha 13 anni*.	ah 13 ahnnee

 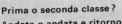

Prima o seconda classe?	First or second class?
Andata o andata e ritorno?	Single or return (one-way or roundtrip)?
Quanti anni ha il bambino/ la bambina?	How old is he/she?

---

* In Italy children between 4 and 12 years of age pay half fare.

All aboard

Is this the right platform for the train to Bellinzona?	È il binario giusto per il treno che va a Bellinzona?	ai eel beenarreeoa joostoa pair eel traynoa kay vah ah behlleendzoanah
Is this the right train to Genoa?	È il treno giusto per Genova?	ai eel trayno joostoa pair jainoavah
Excuse me. May I get by?	Mi scusi. Posso passare?	mee skoozee. posssoa pahsssarray
Is this seat taken?	È occupato questo posto?	ai oakkoopartoa kooaystoa postoa

> **VIETATO FUMARE**
> NO SMOKING

I think that's my seat.	Penso che questo sia il mio posto.	paynsoa kay kooaystoa seeah eel meeoa postoa
Would you let me know before we get to Milan?	Può avvisarmi prima di arrivare a Milano?	pwo ahvveezarrmee preemah dee ahrreevahray ah meelarnoa
What station is this?	Che stazione è?	kay stahtseeoanay ai
How long does the train stop here?	Quanto tempo si ferma qui il treno?	kwahntoa tehmpoa see fayrmah kooee eel traynoa
When do we get to Pisa?	Quando arriveremo a Pisa?	kwahndoa ahrreevay-raymoa ah peezah

Sometime on the journey the ticket collector (*il controllore*—koantroalloaray) will come around and say: *Biglietti, per favore* (Tickets, please)!

Eating

If you want a full meal in the dining-car, you may have to get a ticket from the attendant who will come round to your compartment. There are usually two sittings for breakfast, lunch and dinner.

You can get snacks and drinks in the buffet-car and in the dining-car when it isn't being used for main meals. On some trains an attendant comes around with snacks, tea, coffee and soft drinks. At the larger stations there are refreshment carts.

| First/Second call for dinner. | Prima/Seconda chiamata per la cena. | preemah/saykoandah koearmartah pair lah chainah |
| Where's the dining-car? | Dov'è la carrozza ristorante? | doavai lah kahrrottsah reestorahntay |

Sleeping

Are there any free compartments in the sleeping-car?	Ci sono degli scompartimenti liberi nel vagone letto?	chee soanoa dailyee skoampahrteemayntee leebayree nail vargonay lehttoa
Where's the sleeping-car?	Dov'è il vagone letto?	doavai eel vahgonay lehttoa
Where's my berth?	Dov'è la mia cuccetta?	doavai lah meeah kootchehttah
Compartments 18 and 19, please.	Gli scompartimenti 18 e 19, per favore.	lyee skoampahrteemayntee 18 eh 19 pair fahvoaray
I'd like a lower berth.	Vorrei la cuccetta inferiore.	vorraiee lah kootchettah eenfayreeoray
Would you make up our berths?	Può preparare le nostre cuccette?	pwo praypahrraray lay nostray kootchehttay
Would you call me at 7 o'clock?	Può svegliarmi alle 7?	pwo svaylyarmee ahllay 7
Would you bring me some coffee in the morning?	Può portarmi un caffè domani mattina?	pwo portahrmee oon kahffay doamarnee mahtteenah

Baggage and porters

Porter!	Facchino!	fahkkeenoa
Can you help me with my bags?	Può prendere le mie borse?	pwo prehndayray lay meeay borsay
Please put them down here.	Per favore, le metta laggiù.	pair fahvoaray lay mayttah lahdjoo

Note: If you want to put them in the guard's van (baggage car), you should register them 24 hours in advance.

FOR PORTERS, also see page 24

TRAVELLING AROUND

Lost!

We hope you'll have no need for the following phrases on your trip... but just in case:

Where's the lost-property (lost- and-found) office?	Dove si trova l'ufficio oggetti smarriti?	doavay see trawvah loof-feecheeoa odjehttee smahrreetee
I've lost...	Ho perso...	oa pehrsoa
this morning yesterday	questa mattina ieri	kooaystah mahtteenah eeairee
I lost it in...	L'ho perso in...	loa pehrsoa een
It's very valuable.	È di molto valore.	ai dee moaltoa vahloaray

Underground (subway)

The *metropolitana* in Rome and Milan corresponds to the London underground or the New York subway. A map showing the various lines and stations is displayed outside every station and in every train compartment. The stations are indicated outside by a red M.

The fare is always the same, irrespective of the distance you travel. The *metropolitana* runs from 5.30 a.m. to 12.30 a.m.

Where's the nearest underground station?	Dove si trova la più vicina stazione della metropolitana?	doavay see trawvah lah peeoo veecheenah stahtseeoanay dayllah maytroapoaleetarnah
Does this train go to...?	Questo treno va a...?	kooaystoa traynoa vah ah
Where do I change for...?	Dove cambio per andare a...?	doavay kahmbeeoa pair ahndarray ah
Is the next station...?	La prossima stazione è...?	lah prossseemah stahtseeoanay ai

Bus—Tram (streetcar)

In most buses you pay as you enter. On some rural buses, you may find the driver also acting as the conductor. In Rome and other big cities you can buy a booklet of tickets for regular journeys.

I'd like a booklet of tickets.	Vorrei un blocchetto di biglietti.	vorraiee oon blokkehttoa dee beelyayttee
Where can I get a bus to the Vatican?	Dove posso prendere l'autobus per andare al Vaticano?	doavay posssoa prehndayray lowtoabooss pair ahndarray ahl vahteekarnoa
What bus do I take for the Colosseum?	Quale autobus devo prendere per andare al Colosseo?	kwarlay owtoabooss dayvoa prehndayray pair ahndarray ahl koaloasssaioa
Where's the...?	Dove si trova...?	doavay see trawvah
bus stop	la fermata d'autobus	lah fehrmartah dowtoabooss
terminus	il capolinea	eel kahpoleenayah
When is the...bus to the Lido?	A che ora parte... autobus per il Lido?	ah kay oarah pahrtay... owtoabooss pair eel leedoa
first/last	il primo/l'ultimo	eel preemoa/loolteemoa
next	il prossimo	eel prossseemoa
How often do the buses to Trastevere run?	Ogni quanto tempo passano gli autobus per Trastevere?	oñee kwahntoa tehmpoa pahsssahnoa lyee owtoabooss pair trahstaivayray
How much is the fare to...?	Quanto costa il biglietto per...?	kwahntoa kostah eel beelyayttoa pair
Do I have to change buses?	Devo cambiare autobus?	dayvoa kahmbeearray owtoabooss
How long does the journey take?	Quanto tempo dura il percorso?	kwahntoa tehmpoa doorah eel payrkoarsoa
Will you tell me when to get off?	Può dirmi quando devo scendere?	pwo deermee kwahndoa dayvoa shayndayray

FERMATA D'AUTOBUS	REGULAR BUS STOP
FERMATA A RICHIESTA	STOPS ON REQUEST

I want to get off at the university.	Desidero scendere all'università.	dayzeedayroa shayndayray ahllooneevayrseetah
Please let me off at the next stop.	Per favore, mi faccia scendere alla prossima fermata.	pair fahvoaray mee fahtcheeah shayndayray ahllah prossseemah fehrmartah
May I please have my luggage?	Per favore, mi può dare il mio bagaglio?	pair fahvoaray mee pwo darray eel meeoa bahgarlyeeoa

There are fast long-distance buses which link major cities throughout Italy as well as bus service to out-of-the-way rural areas. You can adapt the phrases in the train section (pages 66–70) to bus travel.

Other means of transport

If you want to visit the Italian islands of Capri, Sardinia or Sicily, you'll find frequent boat service available from the mainland.

Or try one of these to get around:

bicycle	la bicicletta	lah beecheeklehttah
boat	il battello	eel bahttehlloa
houseboat	la "casa galleggiante"	lah karssah gahllaydjeeahntay
motorboat	il motoscafo	eel moatoaskarfoa
rowing-boat	la barca a remi	lah bahrkah ah raimee
sailing-boat	la barca a vela	lah bahrkah ah vaylah
helicopter	l'elicottero	layleekottayroa
hitch-hiking	l'autostop	lowtaostop
horseback riding	cavalcare	kahvahlkarray
hovercraft	il battello su cuscini	eel bahttehlloa soo koosheenee
moped (motor-bike)	la motoretta	lah moatoarehttah
motorcycle	la motociclétta	lah moatoacheeklehttah

Around and about—Sightseeing

Here we're more concerned with the cultural aspect of life than with entertainment; and, for the moment, with towns rather than the countryside. If you want a guide book, ask…

Can you recommend a good guide book for Rome?	Può consigliarmi una buona guida di Roma?	pwo konseelyahrmee oonah bwawnah gooeedah dee roamah
Is there a tourist office?	C'è un ufficio turistico?	chai oon ooffeecheeoa tooreesteekoa
Where's the tourist office/information centre?	Dov'è l'ufficio turistico/l'ufficio informazioni?	doavai looffeecheeoa too-reesteekoa/looffeecheeoa eenfoarmartseeoanee
What are the main points of interest?	Quali sono i principali punti di interesse?	kwahlee soanoa ee preencheeparlee poontee dee eentayraysssay
We're here for…	Siamo qui per…	seearmoa kooee pair
only a few hours	alcune ore soltanto	ahlkoonay oaray soltahntoa
a day	un giorno	oon joarnoa
three days	tre giorni	tray joarnee
a week	una settimana	oonah saytteemarnah
Can you recommend a sightseeing tour?	Può consigliarmi un giro turistico?	pwo konseelyahrmee oon jeeroa tooreesteekoa
Where does the bus start from?	Da dove parte l'autobus?	dah doavay pahrtay lowtoabooss
Will it pick us up at the hotel?	Passerà a prenderci all'albergo?	pahsssayrah ah prehn-dayrchee ahllahlbayrgoa
How much does the tour cost?	Quanto costa l'escursione?	kwahntoa kostah layskoorseeoanay
What time does the tour start?	A che ora si parte per l'escursione?	ah kay oarah see pahrtay pair layskoorseeoanay
What bus/tram (street-car) do we take?	Quale autobus/tram prendiamo?	kwahlay owtoabooss/trahm prehndeearmoa
We'd like to rent a car for the day.	Desideriamo noleggiare un'auto per tutto il giorno.	dayzeedayreearmoa noa-laydjeearray oonowtoa pair toottoa eel joarnoa

FOR TIME OF DAY, see page 179

SIGHTSEEING

SIGHTSEEING

Is there an English-speaking guide?	C'è un cicerone che parla inglese?	chai oon cheechayroanay kay pahrlah eengglayssay
Where is/Where are the...?	Dove si trova/Dove si trovano...?	doavay see trawvah/ doavay see troavahnoa
abbey	l'abbazia	lahbbahtseeah
aquarium	l'acquario	lahkkwarreeoa
amphitheatre	l'anfiteatro	lahnfeetayartroa
art gallery	la galleria d'arte	lah gahllayreeah dahrtay
artists' quarter	il quartiere degli artisti	eel kwahrteeayray daylyee ahrteestee
botanical gardens	i giardini botanici	ee jahrdeenee botar-neechee
building	l'edificio	laydeefeechoa
business district	il quartiere degli affari	eel kwahrteeayray daylyee ahffarree
castle	il castello	eel kahstehlloa
catacombs	le catacombe	lay kartarkombay
cathedral	la cattedrale	lah kahttaydrarlay
cemetery	il cimitero	eel cheemeetairoa
city centre	il centro città	eel chayntroa cheettah
city hall	il municipio	eel mooneecheepeeoa
church	la chiesa	lah keeayzah
coliseum	il colosseo	eel koaloasssayoa
concert hall	la sala dei concerti	lah sarlah daiee kon-chehrtee
convent	il convento	eel konvayntoa
court house	il palazzo di giustizia	eel parlahttsoa dee joosteetseeah
downtown area	il centro città	eel chayntroa cheettah
fortress	la fortezza	lah fortehttsah
fountain	la fontana	lah foantarnah
gardens	i giardini	ee jahrdeenee
grotto	la grotta	lah grottah
harbour	il porto	eel portoa
library	la biblioteca	lah beebleeootaikah
market	il mercato	eel mayrkartoa
memorial	il memoriale	eel maymoareearlay
monastery	il monastero	eel moanahstairoa
monument	il monumento	eel moanoomayntoa
museum	il museo	eel moozaioa
old city	la città vecchia	lah cheettah vehkkeeah
opera house	il teatro dell'opera	eel tayartroa daylloapehrah
palace	il palazzo	eel pahlahttsoa
park	il parco	eel pahrkoa
parliament building	il palazzo del Parlamento	eel pahlahttsoa dayl pahrlarmayntoa

planetarium	il planetario	eel plahnaytarreeoa
presidential palace	il palazzo presidenziale	eel pahlahttsoa prayssee-dayntseearlay
ruins	le rovine	lay roveenay
shopping centre	la zona degli acquisti	lah dzonah daylyee ahkkooeeestee
shrine	il reliquario	eel rayleekwahreeoa
stadium	lo stadio	loa stardeeoa
statue	la statua	lah startooah
stock exchange	la borsa valori	lah borsah vahloaree
supreme court	la Corte Suprema	lah koartay soopraymah
synagogue	la sinagoga	lah seenahgogah
temple	il tempio	eel tehmpeeoa
tomb	la tomba	lah toambah
tower	la torre	lah toarray
university	l'università	looneevayrseetah
vaults	i sotterranei/le cripte	ee soattayrrarnayee/lay kreeptay
zoo	lo zoo	loa dzoaoa

Admission

Is...open on Sundays?	È aperto la domenica il...?	ai ahpehrtoa lah doamay-neekah eel
When does it open?	Quando apre?	kwahndoa arpray
When does it close?	Quando chiude?	kwahndoa keeooday
How much is the entrance fee?	Quanto costa l'entrata?	kwahntoa kostah layntrartah
Is there any reduction for...?	C'è una riduzione per...?	chai oonah reedootseeoaanay pair
students	gli studenti	lyee stoodayntee
children	i bambini	ee bahmbeenee
Have you a guide book (in English)?	Avete una guida (in inglese)?	ahvaytay oonah gooeedah (een eengglayssay)
Can I buy a catalogue?	Posso comperare un catalogo?	posssoa koampayrarray oon kahtarloagoa
Is it all right to take pictures?	È permesso fare delle fotografie?	ai pehrmaysssoa farray dayllay foatoagrahfeeay

---

| ENTRATA LIBERA | ADMISSION FREE |
| VIETATO FOTOGRAFARE | NO CAMERAS ALLOWED |

SIGHTSEEING

Who—What—When?

What's that building?	Che cos'è quest'edificio?	kay kossai kooaystaydeefeechoa
Who was the...?	Chi è stato...?	kee ai startoa
architect	l'architetto	lahrkeetehttoa
artist	l'artista	lahrteestah
painter	il pittore	eel peettoaray
sculptor	lo scultore	loa skooltoaray
Who built it?	Chi lo costruì?	kee loa koastrooee
Who painted that picture?	Chi dipinse questo quadro?	kee deepeensay kooaystoa kwardroa
When did he live?	Quando è vissuto?	kwahndoa ai veesssootoa
When was it built?	Quando fu costruito?	kwahndoa foo koastrooeetoa
Where's the house where...lived?	Dove si trova la casa in cui visse...?	doavay see trawvah lah karssah een kooee veesssay
We're interested in...	Ci interessiamo di...	chee eentayraysssseearmoa dee
antiques	antichità	ahnteekeetah
archaeology	archeologia	ahrkayoaloajeeah
art	arte	ahrtay
botany	botanica	botarneekah
ceramics	ceramiche	chayrarmeekay
coins	monete	monaitay
crafts	artigianato	ahrteejarnartoa
fine arts	belle arti	behllay ahrtee
furniture	mobilio	mobeeleeoa
geology	geologia	jayoaloajeeah
history	storia	storeeah
medicine	medicina	maydeecheenah
music	musica	moozeekah
natural history	storia naturale	storeeah nartoorarlay
ornithology	ornitologia	oarneetoaloajeeah
painting	pittura	peettoorah
pottery	terrecotte	tehrraykottay
prehistory	preistoria	prayeestoreeah
sculpture	scultura	skooltoorah
wild life	flora e fauna	florah ay faroonah
zoology	zoologia	dzoaoaloajeeah
Where's the...department?	Dov'è il reparto di/del...?	doavai eel raypahrtoa dee/dayl

Just the adjective you've been looking for...

It's...	È...	ai
amazing	**sorprendente**	soarprayn**dehn**tay
awful	**spaventoso**	spahvayn**tos**soa
beautiful	**bellissimo**	behl**leess**seemoa
gloomy	**malinconico**	mahleengkoneekoa
impressive	**impressionante**	eempraysssee**oa**nahntay
interesting	**interessante**	eentayrayss**sahn**tay
magnificent	**magnifico**	mah**ñee**feekoa
monumental	**monumentale**	moanoomayn**tar**lay
overwhelming	**sbalorditivo**	sbahloardee**tee**voa
sinister	**sinistro**	see**nees**troa
strange	**strano**	**strar**noa
superb	**superbo**	soo**pehr**boa
terrible	**terribile**	tayr**ree**beelay
terrifying	**terrificante**	tayrreefee**kahn**tay
tremendous	**fantastico**	fahn**tah**steekoa
ugly	**brutto**	**broot**toa

Religious services

Most churches and cathedrals are open to the public, except, of course, during mass.

If you are interested in taking pictures, you should obtain permission first. Shorts and backless dresses are definitely out when visiting churches.

Is there a/an...near here?	C'è una...qui vicino?	chai **oo**nah...koo**ee** vee**chee**noa
Catholic church	**chiesa cattolica**	kee**ay**zah kaht**toa**leekah
Protestant church	**chiesa protestante**	kee**ay**zah proatay**stahn**tay
synagogue	**sinagoga**	seenah**gog**ah
mosque	**moschea**	moa**skai**ah
At what time is...?	A che ora è...?	ah kay **oa**rah ai
mass	**la messa**	lah **mayss**sah
the service	**la funzione**	lah foont**see**oonay
Where can I find a ...who speaks English?	Dove posso trovare un...che parla inglese?	**doa**vay **poss**soa trawvar-ray oon...kay **pahr**lah eeng**glay**ssay
priest/minister	**prete/pastore**	**prai**tay/pah**stoa**ray
rabbi	**rabbino**	rahb**bee**noa

Relaxing

Cinema (movies)—Theatre

Cinema showings are usually continuous. The matinée usually starts around 2 p.m. There's generally an intermission midway through the feature film.

Theatres close one day a week but give matinées on Sundays. They start later than at home. Booking in advance is advisable.

You can find out what's playing from newspapers and billboards. In most large towns you'll find publications of the type "This Week in..."

Have you a copy of "This Week in..."?	**Ha la rivista "Questa settimana in..."?**	ah lah reeveestah kooaystah saytteemarnah een...
What's showing at the cinema tonight?	**Cosa danno al cinema questa sera?**	kawssah dahnnoa ahl cheenaymah kooaystah sayrah
What's playing at the...theatre?	**Che spettacolo c'è al teatro...?**	kay spayttarkoaloa chai ahl tayartroa
What sort of play is it?	**Che genere di opera è?**	kay jainayray dee opayrah ai
Who's it by?	**Di chi è?**	dee kee ai
Can you recommend (a)...?	**Può consigliarmi...?**	pwo konseelyahrmee
good film	**un buon film**	oon bwawn film
comedy	**una commedia**	oonah koammaideeah
something amusing	**qualcosa di divertente**	kwahlkawssah dee deevayrtainteh
drama	**un dramma**	oon drahmmah
musical	**un'operetta**	oonopayrehttah
revue	**una rivista**	oonah reeveestah
thriller	**un giallo**	oon jahlloa
Western	**un Western**	oon "western"
At what theatre is that new play by... being performed?	**In quale teatro viene rappresentata la nuova opera teatrale di...?**	een kwarlay tayartroa veeaynay rahpprayssayntartah lah nwawvah opayrah tayahtrarlay dee

Where's that new film by... being shown?	Dov'è proiettato il nuovo film di...?	doavai proaeeehttahtoa eel nwawvoa film dee
Who's in it?	Chi sono gli attori?	kee soanoa lyee ahttoaree
Who's playing the lead?	Chi è l'attore principale?	kee ai lahttoaray preencheeparlay
Who's the director?	Chi è il regista?	kee ai eel rayjeestah
What time does it begin?	A che ora incomincia?	ah kay oarah eengkoameencheeah
What time does the show end?	A che ora termina lo spettacolo?	ah kay oarah tehrmeenah loa spayttarkoaloa
What time does the first evening performance start?	A che ora inizia il primo spettacolo serale?	ah kay oarah eeneetseeah eel preemoa spayttarkoaloa sayrarlay
Are there any tickets for tonight?	Ci sono biglietti per questa sera?	chee soanoa beelyayttee pair kooaystah sayrah
How much are the tickets?	Quanto costano i biglietti?	kwahntoa kostarnoa ee beelyayttee
I want to reserve 2 tickets for the show on Friday evening.	Desidero prenotare 2 biglietti per lo spettacolo di venerdì sera.	dayzeedayroa praynoatarray 2 beelyayttee pair loa spayttarkoaloa dee vaynayrdee sayrah
Can I have a ticket for the matinée on Tuesday?	Posso avere un biglietto per lo spettacolo del pomeriggio di martedì?	posssoa ahvayray oon beelyayttoa pair loa spayttarkoaloa dayl poamayreedjoa dee mahrtaydee
I want a seat in the stalls (orchestra).	Desidero una poltrona.	dayzeedayroa oonah poaltroanah
Not too far back.	Non troppo indietro.	noan troppoa eendeeaytroa
Somewhere in the middle.	A metà circa.	ah maytah cheerkah
How much are the seats in the circle (mezzanine)?	Quanto costano i posti in galleria?	kwahntoa kostahnoa ee postee een gahllayreeah
May I please have a programme?	Per favore, posso avere un programma?	pair fahvoaray posssoa ahvayray oon programhmah
Can I check this coat?	Posso depositare questo cappotto?	posssoa daypoasseetarre kooaystoa kahppottoa

RELAXING

Sono spiacente, è tutto esaurito.	I'm sorry, we're sold out.
Vi sono solo alcuni posti in galleria.	There are only a few seats left in the circle (mezzanine).
Posso vedere il suo biglietto?*	May I see your ticket?*
Questo è il suo posto.	This is your seat.

Opera—Ballet—Concert

Where's the opera house?	Dov'è il teatro dell'opera?	doavai eel tayartroa dayllopayrah
Where's the concert hall?	Dov'è la sala dei concerti?	doavai lah sarlah daiee koanchehrtee
What's on at the opera tonight?	Quale spettacolo c'è all'Opera questa sera?	kwahlay spayttarkoaloa chai ahllopayrah kooaystah sayrah
Who's singing?	Chi canta?	kee kahntah
Who's dancing?	Chi balla?	kee bahllah
What time does the programme start?	A che ora inizia il programma?	ah kay oarah eeneetseeah eel programmah
What orchestra is playing?	Che orchestra suona?	kay oarkaystrah swonah
What are they playing?	Cosa suonano?	kawssah swonahnoa
Who's the conductor?	Chi è il maestro?	kee ai eel mahehstroa

---

* It's customary at the theatre to give a small tip to the usherette after she has shown you to your seat.

Night-clubs

Night-clubs—with dinner, dancing and a floor show—are found only in major cities and popular spas. But you'll certainly want to experience the informal atmosphere of a *bodega* or *taberna*. Some of them are found in candlelit cellars or in bars where a tiny space has been set aside for entertainment. While sipping a sherry or Spanish brandy, you might watch fiery flamenco dancing or listen to melancholy guitar music.

In holiday resorts along the coast, a lot of *bodegas* are made for the tourist trade; entertainment may be keyed to appeal to foreigners who'll pay high prices for it. But ask around for good *bodegas* and *tabernas* for a more authentic style of singing, dancing and music that the Spaniards enjoy.

Can you recommend a good night-club?	¿Puede recomen-darme una buena sala de fiestas?	pwaydhay raykoamayn-dahrmay oonah bwaynah sahlah day fyaystahss
Is there a floor show?	¿Hay atracciones?	igh ahtrahkthyonayss
What time does the floor show start?	¿A qué hora empiezan las atracciones?	ah kay oarah aympyay-thahn lahss ahtrahkthyo-nayss
Is evening attire necessary?	¿Se necesita traje de noche?	say naythaysseetah trahkhay day noachay

And once inside...

A table for 2, please.	Una mesa para 2, por favor.	oonah mayssah pahrah 2 por fahbhor
My name's...I reserved a table for 4.	Mi nombre es...He reservado una mesa para 4.	mee noambray ayss...ay rayssehrbahdhoa oonah mayssah pahrah 4
I telephoned you earlier.	Le he telefoneado antes.	lay ay taylayfoanehahdhoa ahntayss
We haven't got a reservation.	No hemos reservado.	noa aymoass rayssehr-bahdhoa

RELAXING

There's a dance at the...	**C'è un ballo al...**	chai oon **bahl**loa ahl
Would you like to dance?	**Vuole ballare?**	vwawlay bahl**lar**ray
May I have this dance?	**Mi concede questo ballo?**	mee koan**cheh**day kooaystoa **bahl**loa

Do you happen to play...?

On a rainy day, this page may solve your problems.

Do you happen to play chess?	**Sa giocare a scacchi?**	sah joa**kar**ray ah **skahk**kee
I'm afraid I don't.	**No, mi dispiace.**	noa mee deespee**ar**chay
No, but I'll give you a game of draughts (checkers).	**No, ma posso fare una partita a dama.**	noa mah **pos**soa **far**ray oonah pahr**tee**tah ah **dar**mah

king	**il re**	eel ray
queen	**la regina**	lah ray**jee**nah
castle (rook)	**la torre**	lah **toar**ray
bishop	**l'alfiere**	lahlfee**ay**ray
knight	**il cavallo**	eel kah**vahl**loa
pawn	**la pedina**	lah pay**dee**nah

| Checkmate! | **Scacco matto!** | **skahk**koa **maht**toa |

| Do you play cards? | **Gioca a carte?** | joakah ah **kahr**tay |

bridge	**bridge**	"bridge"
canasta	**canasta**	kar**nah**stah
gin rummy	**ramino**	rah**mee**noa
whist	**whist**	"whist"
pontoon (21)	**tressette**	trays**sait**tay
poker	**poker**	"poker"

ace	**l'asso**	**lahs**soa
king	**il re**	eel ray
queen	**la regina**	lah ray**jee**nah
jack	**il fante**	eel **fahn**tay
joker	**la matta/il jolly**	lah **maht**tah/eel jolly

hearts	**cuori**	**kwaw**ree
diamonds	**quadri**	**kwar**dree
clubs	**fiori**	fee**oa**ree
spades	**picche**	**peek**kay

RELAXING

Casino and gambling

Italy's casinos are all located in the northern part of the country—Campione near Como, the Lido near Venice, San Remo on the Italian Riviera and St. Vincent in the Aosta Valley.

To get into a casino, you'll need your passport. (You must be over 21.) You must also have a "clean record" in the gambling world. For your part, you need have no doubts about the honesty of the game. All legitimate casinos are strictly controlled and regularly inspected. Casinos are anxious to avoid any risk of scandal or adverse public relations.

Entrance fees are nominal. The language of the casino is mostly French, but the croupiers will understand enough English for your requirements.

In addition there are horse and dog races where parimutuel bets are accepted. Italians play *totocalcio* with a passion. This is government-operated betting on the final scores of football games. Another popular game of chance is the weekly state lottery.

RELAXING

Sports

Italians love action sports like football (soccer) and motorcycle and speedboat racing. There are also horse shows, golf and tennis tournaments, water polo, trotting races and boating. For your own recreation you'll be able to go fishing, golfing, skin diving, swimming or play a round of tennis.

| Where's the nearest golf course? | Dove si trova il campo da golf più vicino? | doavay see trawvah eel kahmpoa dah golf peeoo veecheenoa |
| Can we hire (rent) clubs? | Possiamo noleggiare le mazze? | possseearmoa noalaydjarray lay mahttsay |

Where are the tennis courts?	Dove sono i campi da tennis?	doavay soanoa ee kahm-pee dah "tennis"
Can I hire rackets?	Posso noleggiare le racchette?	posssoa noalaydjeearray lay rahkkehttay
What's the charge per...?	Qual è il prezzo per...?	kwahl ai eel prehttsoa pair
day/round/hour	un giorno/una partita/un'ora	oon joarnoa/oonah pahrteetah/oonoarah
Where's the nearest race course (track)?	Dov'è l'ippodromo più vicino?	doavai leeppoadromoa peeoo veecheenoa
What's the admission charge?	Quanto costa l'entrata?	kwahntoa kostah layntrartah
Is there a swimming pool here?	C'è una piscina qui?	chai oonah peesheenah kooee
Is it open-air or indoors?	È una piscina all'aperto o coperta?	ai oonah peesheenah ahllahpehrtoa oa koapehrtah
Is it heated?	È riscaldata?	ai reeskahldahtah
Can one swim in the lake/river?	Si può nuotare nel lago/fiume?	see pwo nwawtarray nayl largoa/feeoomay
I'd like to see a boxing match.	Vorrei vedere un incontro di pugilato.	vorraiee vaydayray oon eengkoantroa dee poojeelartoa
Can you get me a couple of tickets?	Può procurarmi un paio di biglietti?	pwo proakoorahrmee oon pareeoa dee beelyayttee
Is there a football (soccer) match anywhere this Saturday?	C'è una partita di calcio da qualche parte, sabato?	chai oonah pahrteetah dee kahlchoa dah kwahlkay pahrtay sarbahtoa
Who's playing?	Chi gioca?	kee joakah
Is there any good fishing around here?	Ci sono buone possibilità di pesca in questa zona?	chee soanoa bwawnay possseebeeleetah dee payskah een kooaystah dzoanah
Do I need a permit?	È necessario il permesso?	ai naychaysssarreeoa eel payrmaysssoa
Where can I get one?	Dove posso procurarmene uno?	doavay posssoa proakoo-rahrmaynay oonoa

On the beach

Is it safe for swimming?	**Si può nuotare senza pericolo?**	see pwo nwawtarray sayntsah payreekoaloa
Is there a lifeguard?	**C'è un bagnino?**	chai oon bahñeenoa
Is it safe for children?	**È sicuro per i bambini?**	ai seekooroa pair ee bahmbeenee
There are some big waves.	**Ci sono cavalloni.**	chee soanoa kahvahlloanee
Are there any dangerous currents?	**Vi sono correnti pericolose?**	vee soanoa koarrayntee payreekoaloassay
What time is high tide?	**A che ora è l'alta marea?**	ah kay oarah ai lahltah marrayah
What time is low tide?	**A che ora è la bassa marea?**	ah kay oarah ai lah bahssah marrayah
What's the temperature of the water?	**Qual è la temperatura dell'acqua?**	kwahl ai lah taympayrahtoorah dayllahkkwah
I want to hire a/an...	**Vorrei noleggiare...**	vorraiee noalaydjarray
air mattress	**un materassino pneumatico**	oon mahtayrahsssseenoa pnayoomarteekoa
bathing hut	**una cabina**	oonah kahbeenah
deck-chair	**una sedia a sdraio**	oonah saydeeah ah sdrareeoa
skin-diving equipment	**un equipaggiamento subacqueo**	oon aykooeepahdjahmayntoa soobahkkooayoa
sunshade	**un ombrellone**	oon oambraylloanay
surf board	**un sandolino**	oon sahndoaleenoa
tent	**una tenda**	oonah taindah
some water-skis	**degli sci nautici**	daylyee shee nowteechee
Where can I rent a...?	**Dove posso noleggiare una...?**	doavay posssoa noalaydjarray oonah
canoe	**canoa**	kaʃnoah
motor-boat	**barca a motore**	bahrkah ah motoaray
rowing-boat	**barca a remi**	bahrkah ah raymee
sailing-boat	**barca a vela**	bahrkah ah vailah
What's the charge per hour?	**Quanto costa all'ora?**	kwahntoa kostah ahlloarah

RELAXING

SPIAGGIA PRIVATA
PRIVATE BEACH

VIETATO FARE IL BAGNO
NO BATHING

Winter sports

While one doesn't think of going skiing in sunny Italy, it is possible particularly in winter. There are a number of ski resorts in the Dolomite Alps and the Piedmont region in northern Italy. Surprisingly, one could also ski at Terminello, not far from Rome, or on Mount Aetna in Sicily.

Is there a skating-rink near here?	C'è una pista di pattinaggio qui vicino?	chai oonah peestah dee pahtteenadjoa kooee veecheenoa
I want to hire some skates.	Vorrei noleggiare dei pattini.	vorraiee noalaydjarray daiee pahtteenee
What are the skiing conditions like at Cortina d'Ampezzo?	Come sono le condizioni per sciare a Cortina d'Ampezzo?	koamay soanoa lay kondeetseeoanee pair sheearray ah koarteenah dahmpehttsoa
Can I take skiing lessons there?	Posso prendere delle lezioni di sci?	posssoa prehndayray dayllay laytseeoanee dee shee
Are there ski lifts?	Ci sono delle sciovie?	chee soanoa dayllay sheeoveeai
I want to hire a/some...	Vorrei noleggiare...	vorraiee noalaydjarray
ice skates	dei pattini	daiee pahtteenee
skiing equipment	una tenuta da sci	oonah taynootah dah shee
toboggan	un toboga	oon tawboagah
sled	una slitta	oonah sleettah
boots	degli scarponi da sci	daylyee skahrpoanee dah shee
poles	dei bastoni	daiee bahstoanee
skis	degli sci	daylyee shee

Camping—Countryside

Camping isn't allowed without a permit in many parts of Italy. However, there are many authorized camping sites with excellent facilities. If you want to be on the safe side, go to one that's recognized by the Italian Touring Association (TCI).

Can we camp here?	Possiamo accamparci qui?	possseearmoa ahkkahmpahrchee kooee
Where can one camp for the night?	Dove possiamo campeggiare questa notte?	doavay possseearmoa kahmpaydjarray kooaystah nottay
Is there a camping site near here?	C'è una zona di campeggio qui vicino?	chai oonah dzoanah dee kahmpaydjoa kooee veecheenoa
May we camp in your field?	Possiamo accamparci nel suo campo?	possseearmoa ahkkahmpahrchee nayl soooa kahmpoa
Can we park our caravan (trailer) here?	Possiamo parcheggiare qui la nostra roulotte?	possseearmoa pahrkaydjarray kooee lah nostrah roolot
Is this an official camping site?	È una zona di campeggio autorizzata?	ai oonah dzoanah dee kahmpaydjoa owtoareeddzartah
May we light a fire?	Possiamo accendere un fuoco?	possseearmoa ahtchehndayray oon fwawkoa
Is there drinking water?	C'è acqua potabile?	chai ahkkwah poatarbeelay
What are the facilities?	Quali sono le facilitazioni?	kwarlee soanoa lay fahcheeleetartseeoanee
Are there shopping facilities on the site?	Ci sono possibilità d'acquisti sul posto?	chee soanoa possseebeeleetah dahkkooeestee sool poastoa
Are there...?	Ci sono...?	chee soanoa
baths	i bagni	ee barñee
showers	le docce	lay dotchay
toilets	i gabinetti	ee gahbeenayttee

What's the charge...?	**Quanto si paga...?**	kwahntoa see pargah
per day	**al giorno**	ahl joarnoa
per person	**per persona**	pair payrsoanah
for a car	**per una macchina**	pair oonah mahkkeenah
for a tent	**per una tenda**	pair oonah taindah
for a caravan (trailer)	**per una roulotte**	pair oonah roolot
Is there a youth hostel near here?	**C'è un ostello della gioventù qui vicino?**	chai oon oastehlloa dayl-lah joavayntoo kooee veecheenoa
Do you know anyone who can put us up for the night?	**Conosce qualcuno che può alloggiarci per questa notte?**	koanoashay kwahlkoonoa kay pwo ahllodjahrchee pair kooaystah nottay

VIETATO CAMPEGGIARE	ROULOTTE VIETATE
NO CAMPING	NO CARAVANS (TRAILERS)

Landmarks

CAMPING

barn	**la baracca**	lah bahrahkkah
bridge	**il ponte**	eel poantay
brook	**il ruscello**	eel rooshehlloa
building	**l'edificio**	laydeefeecheeoa
canal	**il canale**	eel kahnarlay
church	**la chiesa**	lah keeaizah
cliff	**la scogliera**	lah skoalyayrah
copse	**il boschetto**	eel boaskehttoa
cornfield	**il campo di grano**	eel kahmpoa dee grarnoa
cottage	**il villino**	eel veelleenoa
crossroads	**l'incrocio**	leengkroachoa
farm	**la fattoria**	lah fahttoareeah
ferry	**il traghetto**	eel trahgehttoa
field	**il campo**	eel kahmpoa
footpath	**il sentiero**	eel saynteeayroa
forest	**la foresta**	lah fawrehstah
hamlet	**il gruppo di casolari**	eel grooppoa dee kahssoalarree
heath	**la brughiera**	lah broogeeayrah
highway	**l'autostrada**	lowtoastrardah
hill	**la collina**	lah koalleenah
house	**la casa**	lah karssah
inn	**la locanda**	lah loakahndah
jungle	**la giungla**	lah joonglah
lake	**il lago**	eel largoa
marsh	**la palude**	lah pahlooday

moorland	la landa	lah **lahn**dah
mountain	la montagna	lah moan**tarñah**
mountain range	la catena di montagne	lah kah**tay**nah dee moan**tarñay**
path	il viottolo	eel vee**ott**oaloa
peak	il picco	eel **peek**koa
plantation	la piantagione	lah peeahntah**joa**nay
pond	lo stagno	loa **starñ**oa
pool	la piscina	lah pee**shee**nah
railway	la ferrovia	lah fehrroa**vee**ah
river	il fiume	eel fee**oo**may
road	la strada	lah **strar**dah
sea	il mare	eel **mar**ray
spring	la sorgente	lah soar**jayn**tay
stream	il torrente	eel toar**rehn**tay
swamp	l'acquitrino	lahkkooee**tree**noa
track	la pista	lah **pees**tah
tree	l'albero	**lahl**bayroa
valley	la valle	lah **vahl**lay
village	il villaggio	eel veel**lahdj**eeoa
vineyard	la vigna	lah **veeñ**ah
water	l'acqua	**lahkk**wah
waterfall	la cascata	lah kah**skar**tah
well	il pozzo	eel **poatt**soa
wood	il bosco	eel **boas**koa

CAMPING

VIETATO L'INGRESSO
NO TRESPASSING

What's the name of that river?	**Come si chiama quel fiume?**	**koa**may see kee**ar**mah koo**oayl** fee**oo**may
How high is that mountain?	**Quanto è alta quella montagna?**	**kwahn**toa ai **ahl**tah koo**oayl**lah moan**tarñah**
Is there a scenic route to...?	**C'è una strada panoramica per...?**	chai **oo**nah **strar**dah pahnoarar**mee**kah pair

...and if you're tired of walking, you can always try hitch-hiking—though you may have to wait a long time for a lift.

| Can you give me a lift to...? | **Può darmi un passaggio fino a...?** | pwo **dahr**mee oon pahsssahdjeeoa **fee**noa ah |

FOR ASKING THE WAY, see page 144

Making friends

Introductions

Here are a few phrases to get you started:

How do you do?	**Molto lieto.**	moaltoa leeaytoa
How are you?	**Come sta?**	koamay stah
Very well, thank you.	**Benissimo, grazie.**	baineessseemoa **grar-tseeay**
How's life?	**Come va?**	koamay vah
Fine, thanks. And you?	**Bene, grazie. E lei?**	bainay grartseeay. ay laiee
May I introduce Miss Philips?	**Posso presentarle la signorina Philips?**	posssoa prayzayntarrlay lah seeñoareenah Philips
I'd like you to meet a friend of mine.	**Vorrei che conoscesse un mio amico.**	vorraiee kay koanoashaysssay oon meeoa ahmeekoa
John, this is...	**John, ti presento...**	"john" tee prayzayntoa
My name's...	**Mi chiamo...**	mee keearmoa
Glad to know you.	**Lieto di fare la sua conoscenza.**	leeaytoa dee farray lah swah koanoashehntsah

Follow-up

How long have you been here?	**Da quanto tempo è qui?**	dah kwahntoa tehmpoa ai kooee
We've been here a week.	**Siamo qui da una settimana.**	seearmoa kooee dah oonah saytteemarnah
Is this your first visit?	**È la prima volta che viene?**	ai lah preemah voltah kay veeaynay
No, we came here last year.	**No, siamo già venuti l'anno scorso.**	noa seearmoa jah vaynootee lahnnoa skoarsoa
Are you enjoying your stay?	**Le piace il suo soggiorno?**	lay peearchay eel swoa soadjoarnoa
Yes, I like...very much.	**Sì, ...mi piace molto.**	see...mee peearchay moaltoa
Are you on your own?	**È solo/sola?**	ai soaloa/soalah

I'm with…	**Sono con…**	soanoa kon
my wife	**mia moglie**	meeah moalyay
my husband	**mio marito**	meeoa mahreetoa
my family	**la mia famiglia**	lah meeah fahmeelyah
my parents	**i miei genitori**	ee meeehee jayneetoaree
some friends	**degli amici**	daylyee ahmeechee
Where do you come from?	**Da dove viene?**	dah doavay veeaynay
What part of…do you come from?	**Da che parte della…viene?**	dah kay pahrtay dayllah… veeaynay
I'm from…	**Sono di…**	soanoa dee
Where are you staying?	**Dove soggiorna?**	doavay soadjoarnah
I'm a student.	**Sono studente.**	soanoa stoodehntay
What are you studying?	**Che cosa studia?**	kay kawssah stoodeeah
We're here on holiday.	**Siamo qui in vacanza.**	seearmoa kooee een vahkahntsah
I'm here on a business trip.	**Sono qui in viaggio d'affari.**	soanoa kooee een veeahdjoa dahffarree
What kind of business are you in?	**Di che genere d'affari si occupa?**	dee kay jaynayray dahffarree see oakkoopah
I hope we'll see you again soon.	**Spero di rivederla presto.**	spayroa dee reevaydehrlah prehstoa
See you later.	**A più tardi.**	ah peeoo tahrdee
See you tomorrow.	**A domani.**	ah domarnee

The weather

They talk about the weather just as much in Italy as the British and Americans are supposed to do. So…

What a lovely day!	**Che bella giornata!**	kay behllah joarnartah
What awful weather.	**Che tempo orribile.**	kay tehmpoa oarreebeelay
Isn't it cold today?	**Che freddo fa oggi, vero?**	kay frehddoa fah odjee vehroa
Isn't it hot today?	**Che caldo fa oggi, vero?**	kay kahldoa fah odjee vehroa

Is it usually as warm as this?	Fa sempre caldo così?	fah saympray kahldoa kawssee
It's very foggy, isn't it?	È molto nebbioso, vero?	ai moaltoa naybbeeoazoa vehroa
Do you think it'll... tomorrow?	Pensa che domani...?	paynsah kay domarnee
rain/snow	pioverà/nevicherà	peeovayrah/nayveekayrah
clear up	si schiarirà	see skeeahreerah
be sunny	ci sarà il sole	chee sahrah eel soalay

Invitations

My wife and I would like you to dine with us on...	Mia moglie e io saremmo lieti di averla a cena da noi il...	meeah moalyay ay eeoa sarrehmmoa leeaytee dee ahvayrlah ah chainah dah noaee eel
Can you come to dinner tomorrow night?	Viene a cena domani sera?	veeaynay ah chainah domarnee sayrah
We're giving a small party tomorrow night. I do hope you can come.	Faremo una festicciola domani sera. Spero veramente che possa venire.	fahraymoa oonah faysteetcholah domarnee sayrah. spayroa vayrahmayntay kay poasssah vayneeray
Can you come over for cocktails this evening?	Viene a un cocktail questa sera?	veeaynay ah oon "cocktail" kooaystah sayrah
There's a party. Are you coming?	C'è una festicciola. Viene?	chai oonah faysteetcholah. veeaynay
That's very kind of you.	È molto gentile da parte sua.	ai moaltoa jaynteelay dah pahrtay swah
Great. I'd love to come.	Fantastico. Sarei lieto di venire.	fahntahsteekoa. sahrehee leeaytoa dee vayneeray
What time shall we come?	A che ora dobbiamo venire?	ah kay oarah doabbeearmoa vayneeray
May I bring a friend?	Posso portare un amico?	posssoa portarray oon ahmeekoa
May I bring my girl friend?	Posso portare la mia ragazza?	posssoa portarray lah meeah rahgahttsah

I'm afraid we've got to go now.	**Mi dispiace, ma adesso dobbiamo andare.**	mee deespeeearchay mah ahdehsssoa doabbeeearmoa alhndarray
Next time you must come to visit us.	**La prossima volta dovete venire da noi.**	lah prossseemah voltah doavaytay vayneeray dah noaee
Thanks for the evening. It was great.	**Grazie per la serata. È stata splendida.**	grartseeay pair la sayrartah. ai startah splehndeedah

Dating

Would you like a cigarette?	**Posso offrirle una sigaretta?**	posssoa offreerlay oonah seegahrayttah
Do you have a light, please?	**Ha un fiammifero, per favore?**	ah oon feeahmmeefayroa pair fahvoaray
Can I get you a drink?	**Posso offrirle qualcosa da bere?**	posssoa offreerlay kwahlkawssah dah bayray
Excuse me, could you please help me?	**Scusi, può aiutarmi?**	skoozee pwo ighootarrmee
I'm lost. Can you show me the way to...?	**Mi sono perduto. Può indicarmi la strada per...?**	mee soanoa pehrdootoa. pwo eendeekarrmee lah strardah pair
Are you waiting for someone?	**Aspetta qualcuno?**	ahspayttah kwahlkoonoa
Are you free this evening?	**È libera stasera?**	ai leebayrah stahssayrah
Would you like to go out with me tonight?	**Uscirebbe con me stasera?**	oosheerehbbay kon may stahssayrah
Would you like to go dancing?	**Le piacerebbe andare a ballare?**	lay peeahchayrehbbay ahndarray ah bahllarray
I know a good discotheque.	**Conosco una buona discoteca.**	koanoaskoa oonah bwawnah deeskoataykah
Shall we go to the cinema (movies)?	**Andiamo al cinema?**	ahndeearmoa ahl cheenaymah
Would you like to go for a drive?	**Andiamo a fare un giro in macchina?**	ahndeearmoa ah farray oon jeeroa een mahkkeenah
Where shall we meet?	**Dove possiamo incontrarci?**	doavay possseearmoa eengkontrarrchee

MAKING FRIENDS

I'll pick you up at your hotel.	Passerò a prenderla all'albergo.	pahsssayroa ah prayndayrlah ahllahlbehrgoa
I'll call for you at 8.	Passerò da lei alle 8.	pahsssayroa dal laiee ahllay 8
May I take you home?	Posso accompagnarla a casa?	posssoa ahkkoampahñarrlah ah karssah
Can I see you again tomorrow?	Posso rivederla domani?	posssoa reevaydayrlah doamarnee
Thank you, it's been a wonderful evening.	Grazie, è stata una magnifica serata.	grartseeay ai startah oonah mahñeefeekah sayrartah
I've enjoyed myself tremendously.	Mi sono divertito moltissimo.	mee soanoa deevayrteetoa moalteessseemoa
What's your telephone number?	Qual è il suo numero di telefono?	kwahl ai eel swoa noomayroa dee taylaifoanoa
Do you live alone?	Vive sola?	veevay soalah
What time is your last train?	A che ora parte il suo ultimo treno?	ah kay oarah pahrtay eel swoa oolteemoa traynoa

This shopping guide is designed to help you find what you want with ease, accuracy and speed. It features:

1. a list of all major shops, stores and services (p. 98)

2. some general expressions required when shopping to allow you to be specific and selective (p. 100)

3. full details of the shops and services most likely to concern you. Here you'll find advice, alphabetical lists of items and conversion charts listed under the headings below.

		Page
Bookshop	books, magazines, newspapers, stationery	104
Camping	camping equipment	106
Chemist's (drugstore)	medicine, first-aid, cosmetics, toilet articles	108
Clothing	clothes, shoes, accessories	112
Electrical appliances	radios, tape-recorders, shavers, records	119
Hairdresser's	barber's, ladies' hairdresser's, beauty salon	121
Jeweller's	jewellery, watches, watch repairs	123
Laundry—Dry cleaning	usual facilities	126
Photography	cameras, accessories, films, developing	127
Provisions	this is confined to basic items required for picnics	129
Souvenirs	souvenirs, gifts, fancy goods	131
Tobacconist's	smoker's supplies	132

SHOPPING GUIDE

Shops, stores and services

If you have a pretty clear idea of what you want before you set out, then look under the appropriate heading, pick out the article and find a suitable description for it (colour, material, etc.).

Shop hours in Italy differ from summer to winter. In winter the shops are generally open from 8 a.m. to 7 p.m. with a lunch break between 1 and 3 p.m. During the tourist season, shops open and close later in the afternoon (4 to 8 p.m.).

Some remain open on Sundays but most close a half day during the week—often Monday morning or Thursday afternoon.

Swiss shops are open from 8 a.m. to noon or 12.30 p.m. and from 1.30 to 6.30 or 7 p.m. (Saturdays until 5 p.m.) with half-day closings similar to Italy.

Where's the nearest...?	Dove si trova... più vicino (vicina)?	doavay see trawvah... peeoo veecheenoa (veecheenah)
antique shop	l'antiquario	lahnteekwarreeoa
art gallery	la galleria d'arte	lah gahllayreeah dahrtay
baker's	la panetteria	lah pahnehttayreeah
bank	la banca	lah bahngkah
barber's	il barbiere	eel bahrbeeayray
beauty salon	l'istituto di bellezza	leesteetootoa dee behllehttsah
bookshop	la libreria	lah leebrayreeah
butcher's	la macelleria	lah mahchayllayreeah
chemist's	la farmacia	lah fahrmahcheeah
cobbler	il calzolaio	eel kahltsoalareeoa
confectioner's	la pasticceria	lah pahsteetchayreeah
dairy	la latteria	lah lahttayreeah
delicatessen	la salumeria	lah sahloomayreeah
dentist	il dentista	eel daynteestah
department store	il grande magazzino	eel grahnday mahgahd-dzeenoa
doctor	il dottore	eel doattoaray
dressmaker's	la sartoria per signora	lah sahrtoareeah pair seeñoarah
drugstore	la farmacia	lah fahrmahcheeah

dry cleaner's	la tintoria	lah teentoareeah
fishmonger's	la pescheria	lah payskayreeah
furrier's	la pellicceria	lah paylleetohayreeah
greengrocer's	il negozio di frutta e verdura	eel naygotseeoa dee froottah ay vehrdoorah
grocery	la drogheria	lah drogayreeah
hairdresser's (ladies)	la parrucchiera	lah pahrrookkeeairah
hardware store	il negozio di ferramenta	eel naygotseeoa dee fehrrarmayntah
hospital	l'ospedale	lospaydarlay
jeweller's	la gioielleria	lah joaeeayllayreeah
launderette	la lavanderia automatica	lah lahvahndayreeah owtoamarteekah
laundry	la lavanderia	lah lahvahndayreeah
liquor store	il negozio di liquori	eel naygotseeoa dee leekwoaree
market	il mercato	eel mayrkartoa
newsagent's	il giornalaio	eel joarnahlareeoa
news-stand	l'edicola	laydeekoalah
optician	l'ottico	lotteekoa
photo shop	il negozio d'apparecchi fotografici	eel naygotseeoa dahppahrehkkee foatoagrarfeechee
police station	il posto di polizia	eel poastoa dee poaleetseeah
post office	l'ufficio postale	looffeechoa poastarlay
shoemaker's (repairs)	il calzolaio	eel kahltsoalareeoa
shoe shop	il negozio di scarpe	eel naygotseeoa dee skahrpay
souvenir shop	il negozio di ricordi	eel naygotseeoa dee reekordee
sporting goods shop	il negozio di articoli sportivi	eel naygotseeoa dee ahrteekoalee sporteevee
stationer's	la cartoleria	lah kahrtoalayreeah
supermarket	il supermercato	eel soopairmayrkartoa
telegraph office	l'ufficio telegrafico	looffeechoa taylaygrarfeekoa
tobacconist's	la tabaccheria	lah tahbahkkayreeah
toy shop	il negozio di giocattoli	eel naygotseeoa dee joakahttoalee
travel agent	l'agenzia di viaggi	lahjayntseeah dee veeahdjee
wine merchant's	il vinaio	eel veenareeoa

SHOPPING GUIDE

| SVENDITA | SALE |

General expressions

Here are some expressions which will be useful to yo
when you're out shopping:

Where?

Where's a good...?	**Dov'è un buon...?**	doavai oon bwawn
Where's the nearest...?	**Dov'è il...più vicino?**	doavai eel...peeoo veecheenoa
Where can I find a...?	**Dove posso trovare un...?**	doavay posssoa trawvarray oon
Where's the main shopping area?	**Dov'è la zona principale dei negozi?**	doavai lah dzoanah preencheeparlay daiee
How far is it from here?	**Quanto dista da qui?**	kwahntoa deestah dah kooee
How do I get there?	**Come ci si può arrivare?**	koamay chee see pwo ahrreevarray

Service

Can you help me?	**Può aiutarmi?**	pwo ighootarrmee
I'm just looking around.	**Do soltanto un'occhiata.**	doa soaltahntoa oonokkeeartah
I want...	**Desidero...**	dayzeedayroa
Can you show me some...?	**Può mostrarmi dei...?**	pwo moastrarrmee daiee
Do you have any...?	**Ha dei...?**	ah daiee

That one

Can you show me...?	**Mi può mostrare...?**	mee pwo moastrarray
that/those	**quello/quelli**	kooaylloa/kooayllee
the one in the window/in the display case	**quello in vetrina/sullo scaffale**	kooaylloa een vaytreenah/soolloa skahffarlay
It's over there.	**È laggiù.**	ai lahdjoo

Defining the article

I'd like a… one.	**Ne vorrei un…**	nay vorraiee oon
big	**grande**	**grahn**day
cheap	**economico**	aykoanaw**mee**koa
dark	**scuro**	**skoo**roa
good	**buono**	**bwaw**noa
heavy	**pesante**	pay**ssahn**tay
large	**largo**	**lahr**goa
light (weight)	**leggero**	laydj**ai**roa
light (colour)	**chiaro**	kee**ar**roa
oval	**ovale**	o**var**lay
rectangular	**rettangolare**	rehttahn**go**larray
round	**rotondo**	ro**toan**doa
small	**piccolo**	**peek**koaloa
square	**quadrato**	kwah**drar**toa
sturdy	**forte**	**for**tay

I don't want anything too expensive.	**Non voglio qualcosa di troppo caro.**	noan **vol**yoa kwahl**kaw**ssah dee **trop**poa **kar**roa

Preference

Can you show me some more?	**Me ne può mostrare degli altri?**	may nay pwo moa**strar**ray **day**lyee **ahl**tree
Haven't you anything…?	**Non ha qualcosa…?**	noan ah kwahl**kaw**ssah
cheaper/better	**meno caro/migliore**	**may**noa **kar**roa/**meel**yoaray
larger/smaller	**più largo/più piccolo**	**peeoo lahr**goa/**peeoo peek**koaloa

How much?

How much is this?	**Quanto costa questo?**	**kwahn**toa **kos**tah **koo**aystoa
How much are they?	**Quanto costano?**	**kwahn**toa **kos**tahnoa
I don't understand.	**Non capisco.**	noan kah**pees**koa
Please write it down.	**Per favore, me lo scriva.**	pair fah**voa**ray may loa **skree**vah
I don't want to spend more than… lire.	**Non voglio spendere più di… lire.**	noan **vol**yoa **spehn**dayray **peeoo** dee … **lee**ray

FOR COLOURS, see page 113

SHOPPING GUIDE

Decision

That's just what I want.	È proprio quello che volevo.	ai **prawpreeoa** kooaylloa kay voalayvoa
It's not quite what I want.	Non è ciò che volevo.	noan ai cho kay voalayvoa
No, I don't like it.	No, non mi piace.	noa noan mee peearchay
I'll take it.	Lo prendo.	loa **prayndoa**

Ordering

Can you order it for me?	Può ordinarmelo?	pwo oardeenahrmayloa
How long will it take?	Quanto tempo ci sarà da aspettare?	kwahntoa tehmpoa chee sahrah dah ahspehttarray

Delivery

I'll take it with me.	Lo porto via.	loa portoa veeah
Deliver it to the... Hotel.	Lo consegni all'Albergo...	loa konsayñee ahllahl-bayrgoa
Please send it to this address.	Per favore, lo mandi a questo indirizzo.	pair fahvoaray loa mahndee ah kooaystoa eendeereettsoa
Will I have any difficulty with the customs?	Avrò delle difficoltà alla dogana?	ahvroa dayllay deeffeekoaltah ahllah doagarnah

Paying

How much is it?	Quant'è?	kwahntai
Can I pay by traveller's cheque?	Accettate i traveller's cheque?	ahtchehttartay ee "traveller's cheque"
Do you accept dollars/pounds?	Accettate dei dollari/delle sterline?	ahtchehttartay daiee dollarree/dayllay stayrleenay
Do you accept credit cards?	Accettate carte di credito?	ahtchehttartay kahrtay dee **kraydeetoa**
Haven't you made a mistake in the bill?	Non vi siete sbagliati nel fare il conto?	noan vee seeaytay sbahlyeeartee nayl farray eel koantoa

Anything else?

No, thanks, that's all.	**No grazie, è tutto.**	noa **grats**seeay ai **toot**toa
Yes, I want...	**Sì, desidero...**	see dayzeedayroa
Show me...	**Mi mostri...**	mee **moa**stree
Thank you. Good-bye.	**Grazie. Arrivederci.**	**grats**seeay ahrreevay-**dair**chee

Dissatisfied

Can you please exchange this?	**Può cambiare questo, per favore?**	pwo kahmbee**array** kooaystoa pair fah**voar**ay
I want to return this.	**Desidero rendere questo.**	dayzee**dayroa rayn**dayray kooaystoa
I'd like a refund. Here's the receipt.	**Desidero essere rimborsato. Ecco la ricevuta.**	dayzeedayroa **ehss**sayray reemboar**sar**toa, **ehk**koa lah reechay**voo**tah

---

Posso aiutarla?	Can I help you?
Cosa desidera?	What would you like?
Che...desidera?	What...would you like?
colore/forma qualità/quantità	colour/shape quality/quantity
Mi dispiace, non ne abbiamo.	I'm sorry, we haven't any.
L'abbiamo esaurito.	We're out of stock.
Dobbiamo ordinarglielo?	Shall we order it for you?
Lo porta via o dobbiamo mandarglielo?	Will you take it with you or shall we send it?
Null'altro?	Anything else?
Sono...lire, per favore.	That's...lire, please.
La cassa è laggiù.	The cashier's over there.

SHOPPING GUIDE

Bookshop—Stationer's—News-stand

In Italy, bookshops and stationers' are usually separate shops, though the latter will often sell paperbacks. Newspapers and magazines are sold at news-stands.

Where's the nearest...?	**Dov'è...più vicina?**	doavai...peeoo veecheenah
bookshop	**la libreria**	lah leebrayreeah
stationer's	**la cartoleria**	lah kahrtoalayreeah
news-stand	**l'edicola**	laydeekoalah
Where can I buy an English-language newspaper?	**Dove posso acquistare un giornale in inglese?**	doavay posssoa ahkkooeestarray oon joarnarlay een eengglayssay
I want to buy a/an/ some...	**Desidero comprare...**	dayzeedayroa koamprarray
address book	**un'agenda per gli indirizzi**	oonahjayndah pair lyee eendeereettsee
ball-point pen	**una penna a sfera**	oonah paynnah ah sfayrah
book	**un libro**	oon leebroa
box of paints	**una scatola di colori**	oonah skartoalah dee koaloree
carbon paper	**della carta carbone**	dayllah kahrtah kahrboanay
cellophane tape	**del nastro adesivo**	dayl nahstroa ahdayzeevoa
crayons	**dei pastelli**	daiee pahstehllee
dictionary Italian-English	**un dizionario italiano-inglese**	oon deetseeoanarreeoa eetahleearnoa/ eengglayssay
drawing paper	**della carta da disegno**	dayllah kahrtah dah deessaynoa
drawing pins	**delle puntine da disegno**	dayllay poonteenay dah deessaynoa
envelopes	**delle buste**	dayllay boostay
eraser	**una gomma**	oonah goammah
file	**una lima**	oonah leemah
fountain pen	**una penna stilografica**	oonah paynnah steeloagrarfeekah
glue	**della colla**	dayllah kollah
guide-book	**una guida**	oonah gooeedah
ink black/red/blue	**dell'inchiostro nero/rosso/blu**	daylleengkeeostroa nayroa/roasssoa/bloo
labels	**delle etichette**	dayllay ayteekehttay
magazine	**una rivista**	oonah reeveestah

map	una carta geografica	oonah kahrtah jayoagrarfeekah
map of the town	una pianta della città	oonah peeahntah dayllah cheettah
road map of...	una carta stradale di...	oonah kahrtah strahdarlay dee
newspaper	un giornale	oon joarnarlay
notebook	un taccuino	oon tahkkooeenoa
note paper	della carta da lettere	dayllah kahrtah dah lehttayray
paperback	un libro tascabile	oon leebroa tahskarbeelay
paper napkins	dei tovaglioli di carta	daiee toavahlyoalee dee kahrtah
paste	della colla forte	dayllah kollah fortay
pen	una penna	oonah paynnah
pencil	una matita	oonah mahteetah
pencil sharpener	un temperino	oon taympayreenoa
playing cards	delle carte da gioco	dayllay kahrtay dah jokoa
postcards	delle cartoline	dayllay kahrtoaleenay
refill (for a pen)	un ricambio (per una penna)	oon reekambeeoa (pair oonah paynnah)
rubber	una gomma	oonah goammah
ruler	una riga	oonah reegah
string	dello spago	daylloa spargoa
tissue paper	della carta velina	dayllah kahrtah vayleenah
typewriter ribbon	un nastro per macchina da scrivere	oon nahstroa pair mahkkeenah dah skreevayray
typing paper	della carta per macchina da scrivere	dayllah kahrtah pair mahkkeenah dah skreevayray
wrapping paper	della carta da pacchi	dayllah kahrtah dah pahkkee
writing pad	un blocco per appunti	oon blokkoa pair appoontee
Where's the guidebook section?	Dov'è il reparto delle guide?	doavai eel raypahrtoa dayllay gooeeday
Where do you keep the English books?	Dov'è il reparto dei libri inglesi?	doavai eel raypahrtoa daiee leebree eengglayssee

Camping

Here we're concerned with the equipment you may need.

SHOPPING GUIDE

I'd like a/an/some…	Vorrei…	vorraiee
axe	una scure	oonah skooray
bottle-opener	un apribottiglia	oon ahpreebotteelyah
bucket	un secchio	oon saykkeeoa
butane gas	del gas butano	dayl gaz bootarnoa
camp bed	un letto da campo	oon lehttoa dah kahmpoa
camping equipment	un equipaggiamento da campeggio	oon aykooeepahdjahmayntoa dah kahmpaydjoa
can opener	un apriscatole	oon ahpreeskahtoalay
(folding) chair	una sedia (pieghevole)	oonah saydeeah (peeaygayvoalay)
compass	una bussola	oonah boosssoalah
corkscrew	un cavatappi	oon kahvahtahppee
crockery	delle stoviglie	dayllay stoaveelyay
cutlery	delle posate	dayllay poassartay
deck-chair	una sedia a sdraio	oonah saydeeah ah sdrareeoa
first-aid kit	una cassetta del pronto soccorso	oonah kahsssehttah dayl proantoa soakkoarsoa
flashlight	una lampadina tascabile	oonah lahmpahdeenah tahskarbeelay
frying-pan	una padella	oonah pahdehllah
groundsheet	un telo per il terreno	oon tayloa pair eel tayrraynoa
hammer	un martello	oon mahrtehlloa
hammock	un'amaca	oonarmahkah
kerosene	del kerosene	dayl kayroassaynay
knapsack	uno zaino	oonoa dzaheenoa
lamp	una lampada	oonah lahmpahdah
lantern	una lanterna	oonah lahntehrnah
matches	dei fiammiferi	daiee feeahmmeefayree
mattress	un materasso	oon mahtayrahsssoa
methylated spirits	dell'alcool metilico	dayllahlkoal mayteeleekoa
mosquito net	una zanzariera	oonah zahnzarreeayrah
pail	un secchio	oon saykkeeoa
paraffin	del kerosene	dayl kayroassaynay
picnic case	un cestino da pic-nic	oon chaysteenoa dah "pic-nic"
pressure cooker	una pentola a pressione	oonah payntoalah ah prayssseeoanay
primus stove	un fornello a petrolio	oon foarnehlloa ah paytroaleeoa

rope	della fune	dayllah foonay
rucksack	un sacco da montagna	oon sahkkoa dah moantarñah
saucepan	una casseruola	oonah kahsssayrwoalah
scissors	un paio di forbici	oon pareeoa dee foarbeechee
screwdriver	un cacciavite	oon kahtchahveetay
sleeping bag	un sacco a pelo	oon sahkkoa ah payloa
stewpan	una pentola	oonah payntoalah
stove	una stufa	oonah stoofah
(folding) table	una tavola (pieghevole)	oonah tarvoalah (peeaygayvoalay)
tent	una tenda	oonah tayndah
tent-peg	un picchetto per tenda	oon peekkehttoa pair tayndah
tent-pole	un palo per tenda	oon parloa pair tayndah
thermos flask (bottle)	un termos	oon tehrmoass
tin-opener	un apriscatole	oon ahpreeskartoalay
tongs	un paio di tenaglie	oon pareeoa dee taynarlyay
tool kit	una cassetta attrezzi	oonah kahsssehttah ahttrehttsee
water carrier	un bidone per l'acqua	oon beedoanay pair lahkkwah
wood alcohol	dell'alcool metilico	dayllahlkoal mayteeleekoa

Crockery

beakers (tumblers)	i bicchieri	ee beekkeeairee
cups	le tazze	lay tahttsay
food box	la cassetta per il cibo	lah kahsssehttah pair eel cheeboa
mugs	i boccali	ee boakkarlee
plates	i piatti	ee peeahttee
saucers	i piattini	ee peeahtteenee

Cutlery

forks	le forchette	lay forkehttay
knives	i coltelli	ee koaltehllee
spoons	i cucchiai	ee kookkeeighee
teaspoons	i cucchiaini	ee kookkeeigheenee
(made of) plastic	(di) plastica	(dee) plarsteekah
(made of) stainless steel	(di) acciaio inossidabile	(dee) ahtchigheeoa eenoassseedarbeelay

Chemist's—Drugstore

The Italian chemists' normally don't stock the great range of goods that you'll find in England or the U.S. For example, they don't sell photographic equipment or books. And for perfume, make-up, etc., you must go to a *profumeria* (proafoomay**ree**ah).

You can recognize a chemist's by the sign outside—a green or red cross, illuminated at night. In the window you'll see a notice telling where the nearest all-night chemist's is.

This section is divided into two parts:

1. Pharmaceutical – medicine, first-aid, etc.
2. Toiletry – toilet articles, cosmetics.

General

Where's the nearest (all-night) chemist's?	**Dov'è la farmacia (di turno) più vicina?**	doavai lah fahrmah**chee**ah (dee **toor**noa) peeoo veecheenah
What time does the chemist's open/ close?	**A che ora apre/ chiude la farmacia?**	ah kay oarah arpray/ keeooday lah fahrmah-**chee**ah

Part 1—Pharmaceutical

I want something for...	**Desidero qualcosa per...**	dayzeedayroa kwahl**kaw**ssah pair
a cold	**il raffreddore**	eel rahffrayd**doo**aray
a cough	**la tosse**	lah **toas**ssay
hay fever	**la febbre del fieno**	lah **fayb**bray dayl feeaynoa
a hangover	**un mal di capo**	oon mahl dee **kar**poa
sunburn	**una scottatura solare**	oonah skoattartoorah soalarray
travel sickness	**il mal d'auto**	eel mahl **dow**toa
an upset stomach	**il mal di stomaco**	eel mahl dee **sto**mahkoa
Can you make up this prescription for me?	**Può prepararmi questa ricetta?**	pwo praypah**rarr**mee kooaystah reecheht**tah**
Shall I wait?	**Devo aspettare?**	**day**voa ahspeht**tar**ray

FOR DOCTOR, see page 162

When shall I come back?	Quando devo ritornare?	kwahndoa dayvoa reetoarnarray
Can I get it without a prescription?	Può darmi questa medicina senza ricetta?	pwo darrmee kooaystah maydeecheenah sayntsah reechehttah
Can I have a/an/some...?	Mi può dare...?	mee pwo darray

adhesive tape	dei cerotti	daiee chayrottee
antiseptic cream	della crema anti-settica	dayllah kraimah ahntee-ssehtteekah
aspirin	delle aspirine	dayllay ahspeereenay
bandage	delle bende	dayllay baynday
crepe/gauze	crespate/di garza	krayspartay/dee gahrdzah
castor oil	dell'olio di ricino	dayllawlyoa dee reecheenoa
contraceptives	degli antifecon-dativi	daylyee ahnteefaykoandah-teevee
corn plasters	un callifugo	oon kahlleefoogoa
cotton wool	del cotone idrofilo	dayl koatoanay eedroafeeloa
cough drops	delle gocce per la tosse	dayllay goatchay pair lah toasssay
disinfectant	del disinfettante	dayl deesseenfehttahntay
ear drops	delle gocce per le orecchie	dayllay goatchay pair lay awraykkeeay
eye drops	delle gocce per gli occhi	dayllay goatchay pair lyee okkee
gargle	un liquido per gargarismi	oon leekooeedoa pair gahrgahreesmee
insect repellent	una crema insetti-cida	oonah kraimah eensehttee-cheedah
iodine	della tintura di iodio	dayllah teentoorah dee eeodeeoa
laxative	un lassativo	oon lahsssahteevoa
mouthwash	un disinfettante per la bocca	oon deesseenfehttahntay pair lah boakkah
sanitary napkins	degli assorbenti igienici	daylyee ahsssoarbayntee eejayneechee
sedative	un sedativo	oon saydahteevoa
sleeping pills	dei sonniferi	daiee soanneefayree
sticking plaster	dei cerotti	daiee chayrottee
stomach pills	delle pillole per lo stomaco	dayllay peelloalay pair loa stomahkoa
throat lozenges	delle pasticche per la gola	dayllay pahsteekkay pair lah goalah

Part 2—Toiletry

SHOPPING GUIDE

I'd like a/an/some…	Desidero…	dayzeedayroa
acne-cream	una crema per l'acne	oonah kraimah pair lahknay
after-shave lotion	una lozione dopobarba	oonah loatseeoanay dawpoabahrbah
astringent	un astringente	oonahstreenjayntay
bath essence	un profumo da bagno	oon proafoomoa dah barñoa
cologne	dell'acqua di colonia	dayllahkkwah dee koaloneeah
cream	una crema	oonah kraimah
cleansing cream	una crema detergente	oonah kraimah daytehrjayntay
cuticle cream	una crema per le pellicine	oonah kraimah pair lay paylleecheenay
foundation cream	un fondo tinta	oon foandoa teentah
moisturizing cream	una crema idratante	oonah kraimah eedrahtahntay
night cream	una crema da notte	oonah kraimah dah nottay
deodorant	un deodorante	oon dayoadoarahntay
emery board	una limetta per unghie	oonah leemehttah pair oonggeeay
eye liner	un eye-liner	oon "eye-liner"
eye pencil	una matita per occhi	oonah mahteetah pair okkee
face pack	una maschera di bellezza	oonah mahskayrah dee behllehttsah
face powder	della cipria	dayllah cheepreeah
foot cream	una crema per i piedi	oonah kraimah pair ee peeaydee
hand cream	una crema per le mani	oonah kraimah pair lay marnee
lipsalve	un burro cacao	oon boorroa kahkaroa
lipstick	un rossetto	oon roasssehttoa
lipstick brush	un pennello per il rossetto	oon paynnehllo pair eel roasssehttoa
make-up remover pads	dei tamponi per togliere il trucco	daiee tahmpoanee pair tolyeeray eel trookkoa
nail clippers	un tagliaunghie	oon tahlyahoonggeeay
nail file	una lima da unghie	oonah leemah dah oonggeeay
nail polish	uno smalto per unghie	oonoa smahltoa pair oonggeeay

nail polish remover	dell'acetone	dayllahchaytoanay
nail scissors	un paio di forbicine per le unghie	oon pareeoa dee forbee-cheenay pair lay oonggeeay
perfume	un profumo	oon proafoomoa
powder	della cipria	dayllah cheepreeah
razor	un rasoio	oon rahssoaeeoa
rouge	un belletto	oon behllehttoa
safety pins	delle spille di sicurezza	dayllay speellay dee seekoorayttsah
shampoo	uno shampoo	oonoa "shampoo"
shaving brush	un pennello da barba	oon paynnehlloa dah bahrbah
shaving cream	una crema da barba	oonah kraimah dah bahrbah
soap	del sapone	dayl sahpoanay
sun-tan cream	una crema solare	oonah kraimah soalarray
sun-tan oil	un olio solare	oonawleeoa soalarray
talcum powder	del talco	dayl tahlkoa
tissues	dei fazzolettini di carta	daiee fahttsoalehtteenee dee kahrtah
toilet paper	della carta igienica	dayllah kahrtah eejayneekah
toilet water	dell'acqua di colonia	dayllahkkwah dee koaloneeah
toothbrush	uno spazzolino da denti	oonoa spahttsoaleenoa dah dehntee
toothpaste	un dentifricio	oon daynteefreechoa
tweezers	delle pinzette	dayllay peentsehttay

For your hair

bobby pins	delle forcine	dayllay foarcheenay
brush	una spazzola per capelli	oonah spahttsoalah pair kahpayllee
comb	un pettine	oon paytteenay
curlers	dei bigodini	daiee beegoadeenee
dye	una tintura	oonah teentoorah
grips	delle forcelle	dayllay foarchayllay
lacquer	della lacca	dayllah lahkkah
oil	della brillantina	dayllah breellahnteenah
pins	delle mollette	dayllay moallayttay
rollers	dei bigodini	daiee beegoadeenee
setting lotion	una lozione fissativa	oonah loatseeooanay feesssahteevah
tint	una sfumatura	oonah sfoomahtoorah

Clothing

If you want to buy something specific, prepare yourself in advance. Look at the list of clothing on page 117. Get some idea of the colour, material and size you want. They're all listed on the next few pages.

General

I'd like...	**Vorrei...**	vorraiee
I want...for a 10-year-old boy.	**Desidero...per un bambino di 10 anni.**	dayzeedayroa... pair oon bahmbeenoa dee 10 ahnnee
I want something like this.	**Voglio qualcosa come questo.**	volyoa kwahlkawssah koamay kooaystoa
I like the one in the window.	**Mi piace quello in vetrina.**	mee peearchay kooaylloa een vaytreenah
How much is that per metre?	**Quanto costa al metro?**	kwahntoa kostah ahl maytroa

1 centimetre = 0.39 in.	1 inch = 2.54 cm.	
1 metre = 39.37 in.	1 foot = 30.5 cm.	
10 metres = 32.81 ft.	1 yard = 0.91 m.	

Colour

I want something in...	**Voglio qualcosa di colore...**	volyoa kwahlkawssah dee koaloaray
I want a darker shade.	**Desidero una tonalità più scura.**	dayzeedayroa oonah toanahleetah peeoo skoorah
I want something to match this.	**Voglio qualcosa per ravvivare questo.**	volyoa kwahlkawssah pair rahvveevarray kooaystoa
I don't like the colour.	**Non mi piace il colore.**	noan mee peearchay eel koaloaray

tinta unita	righe	pallini	quadri	fantasia
(teentah ooneetah)	(reegay)	(pahlleenee)	(kwardree)	(fahntahzeeah)

beige	beige	baij
black	nero	nayroa
blue	blu	bloo
brown	marrone	mahrroanay
cream	crema	kraimah
crimson	cremisi	kraimeezee
emerald	smeraldo	smayrahldoa
fawn	fulvo	foolvoa
gold	oro	oroa
green	verde	vayrday
grey	grigio	greejoa
mauve	malva	mahlvah
orange	arancio	arrahnchoa
pink	rosa	rawzah
purple	porporino	poarpoareenoa
red	rosso	roasssoa
scarlet	scarlatto	skahrlahttoa
silver	argento	ahrjayntoa
turquoise	turchese	toorkayzay
white	bianco	beeahngkoa
yellow	giallo	jahlloa

Material

Do you have anything in...?	Ha qualcosa in...?	ah kwahlkawssah een
I want a cotton blouse.	Voglio una blusa di cotone.	volyoa oonah bloossah dee koatoanay
Is that...?	È un prodotto...?	ai oon proadoattoa
hand-made	fatto a mano	fahttoa ah marnoa
imported	importato	eempoartartoa
made here	nazionale	nahtseeoanarlay
I want something thinner.	Desidero qualcosa di più fine.	dayzeedayroa kwahlkawssah dee peeoo feenay
Do you have any better quality?	Ha una qualità migliore?	ah oonah kwahleetah meelyoaray
What's it made of?	Di che cosa è fatto?	dee kay kawssah ai fahttoa

It may be made of…

cambric	il percalle	eel payr**kah**llay
camel-hair	il pelo di cammello	eel **pay**loa dee kahm-**mehl**loa
chiffon	lo chiffon	loa sheef**foan**
corduroy	il velluto a coste	eel vay**lloo**toa ah **koas**tay
cotton	il cotone	eel koa**toa**nay
crepe	il crespo	eel **krays**poa
felt	il feltro	eel **fayl**troa
flannel	la flanella	lah flah**nehl**lah
gabardine	il gabardine	eel gahbahr**deen**
lace	il pizzo	eel **peet**tsoa
leather	la pelle	lah **pehl**lay
linen	il lino	eel **lee**noa
piqué	il picchè	eel peek**kai**
poplin	il popeline	eel poapay**leen**
rayon	il rayon	eel **raree**oan
satin	il raso	eel **rars**soa
serge	la saia	lah **sar**eeah
silk	la seta	lah **say**tah
suede	la renna	lah **rehn**nah
terrycloth	il tessuto di spugna	eel tays**ssoo**toa dee **spoo**ñah
tulle	il tulle	eel **too**llay
tweed	il tweed	eel "tweed"
velvet	il velluto	eel vay**lloo**toa
velveteen	il velluto di cotone	eel vay**lloo**toa dee koa**toa**nay
wool	la lana	lah **lar**nah
worsted	il pettinato	eel paytteen**ar**toa
synthetic	sintetico	seen**tay**teekoa
wash and wear	non si stira	noan see **stee**rah
wrinkle resistant	ingualcibile	eengwahl**chee**beelay

Size

My size is 38.	La mia misura è il 38.	lah **mee**ah mee**zoo**rah ai eel 38
Could you measure me?	Può prendermi le misure?	pwo **prehn**dayrmee lay mee**zoo**ray
I don't know the Italian sizes.	Non conosco le misure italiane.	noan koa**noas**koa lay mee**zoo**ray eetahlee**ar**nay

In that case, look at the charts on the next page.

This is your size

In Europe sizes vary somewhat from country to country, so this table must be taken as an approximate guide.

Ladies

Dresses/Suits					
American	10	12	14	16	18	20
British	32	34	36	38	40	42
Continental	38	40	42	44	46	48

Stockings							Shoes			
American ⎱ British ⎰	8	8½	9	9½	10	10½	6 4½	7 5½	8 6½	9 7½
Continental	0	1	2	3	4	5	37	38	40	41

Gentlemen

Suits/Overcoats						Shirts			
American ⎱ British ⎰	36	38	40	42	44	46	15	16	17	18
Continental	46	48	50	52	54	56	38	41	43	45

Shoes								
American ⎱ British ⎰	5	6	7	8	8½	9	9½	10	11
Continental	38	39	41	42	43	43	44	44	45

A good fit?

Can I try it on?	Posso provarlo?	posssoa provahrloa
Where's the fitting room?	Dov'è la cabina di prova?	doavai lah kahbeenah dee prawvah
Is there a mirror?	C'è uno specchio?	chai oonoa spaykkeeoa
Does it fit?	Va bene?	vah bainay
It fits very well.	Va molto bene.	vah moaltoa bainay

FOR NUMBERS, see page 176

SHOPPING GUIDE

It doesn't fit.	**Non va bene.**	noan vah **bai**nay
It's too...	**È troppo...**	ai **trop**poa
short/long	**corto/lungo**	**koar**toa/**loong**goa
tight/loose	**stretto/largo**	**strayt**toa/**lahr**goa
How long will it take to alter?	**Quanto tempo ci vuole per le modifiche?**	**kwahn**toa **tehm**poa chee **vwo**lay pair lay moa**dee**feekay

Shoes

I'd like a pair of...	**Vorrei un paio di...**	vor**rai**ee oon **pa**reeoa dee
shoes/sandals	**scarpe/sandali**	**skahr**pay/sahn**dah**lee
boots/slippers	**stivali/pantofole**	stee**var**lee/pahn**tof**oalay
These are too...	**Queste sono troppo...**	kooay**stay soa**noa **trop**poa
narrow/wide	**strette/larghe**	**strayt**tay/**lahr**gay
large/small	**grandi/piccole**	**grahn**dee/**peek**koalay
They pinch my toes.	**Mi fanno male alle punte dei piedi.**	mee **fahn**noa **mar**lay **ahl**lay **poon**tay **dai**ee peeaydee
Do you have a larger size?	**Ha un numero più grande?**	ah oon **noo**mayroa peeoo **grahn**day
I want a smaller size.	**Desidero un numero più piccolo.**	day**zee**dayroa oon **noo**mayroa peeoo **peek**koaloa
Do you have the same in...?	**Ha lo stesso in...?**	ah loa **stayss**soa een
brown/beige	**marrone/beige**	mahr**roa**nay/baij
black/white	**nero/bianco**	**nay**roa/bee**ahng**koa
I'd like a shoe polish.	**Vorrei del lucido.**	vor**rai**ee dayl **loo**cheedoa

Shoes worn out? Here's the key to getting them fixed again:

Can you repair these shoes?	**Mi può riparare queste scarpe?**	mee pwo reepah**rar**ray kooay**stay skahr**pay
Can you stitch this?	**Può attaccare questo?**	pwo ahttahk**kar**ray kooay**stoa**
I want new soles and heels.	**Desidero suole e tacchi nuovi.**	day**zee**dayroa **swo**lay ay **tahk**kee **nwaw**vee
When will they be ready?	**Quando saranno pronte?**	**kwahn**doa sah**rahn**noa **proan**tay

Clothes and accessories

I'd like a/an/some...	Vorrei...	vorraiee
anorak	una giacca a vento	oonah jahkkah ah vayntoa
bath robe	un accappatoio	oon ahkkahppahtoaeeoa
bathing cap	una cuffia da bagno	oonah kooffeeah dah barñoa
bathing suit	un costume da bagno	oon koastoomay dah barñoa
blouse	una blusa	oonah bloozah
boots	degli stivali	daylyee steevarlee
bow tie	una cravatta a farfalla	oonah krahvahttah ah fahrfahllah
bra	un reggiseno	oon raydjeessehnoa
braces	delle bretelle	dayllay braytehllay
briefs	delle mutande da uomo	dayllay mootahnday dah womoa
cap	un berretto	oon bayrrayttoa
cardigan	una giacca di lana	oonah jahkkah dee larnah
coat	un soprabito	oon soaprarbeetoa
dinner jacket	uno smoking	oonoa "smoking"
dress	un vestito	oon vaysteetoa
dressing gown	una veste da camera	oonah vehstay dah karmayrah
evening dress (woman's)	un abito da sera	oon arbeetoa dah sayrah
frock	un abito	oon arbeetoa
girdle	un busto	oon boostoa
gloves	dei guanti	daiee gwahntee
handkerchief	un fazzoletto	oon fahddzoalehttoa
hat	un cappello	oon kahppehlloa
jacket	una casacca	oonah kahssahkkah
jeans	dei jeans	daiee "jeans"
jersey	una camicetta a maglia	oonah kahmeechehttah ah marlyah
jumper (Br.)	un maglione	oon mahlyoanay
negligé	un negligé	oon naygleejay
nightdress	una camicia da notte	oonah kahmeechah dah nottay
overalls	una tuta	oonah tootah
panties	dei calzoncini da donna	daiee kahltsoancheenee dah donnah
panty-girdle	un corsetto	oon koarsayttoa
panty hose	dei collant	daiee koallahnt
parka	una giacca a vento	oonah jahkkah ah vayntoa
pinafore	uno scamiciato	oonoa skahmeechahtoa

pyjamas	un pigiama	oon peejarmah
raincoat	un impermeabile	oon eempaymayarbeelay
robe	un mantello	oon mahntehlloa
sandals	dei sandali	daiee sahndahlee
scarf	una sciarpa	oonah shahrpah
shirt	una camicia	oonah kahmeechah
shoes	delle scarpe	dayllay skahrpay
skirt	una gonna	oonah goannah
slip	una sottoveste	oonah soattoavehstay
slippers	delle pantofole	dayllay pahntofoalay
socks	dei calzini	daiee kahltseenee
sports jacket	una giacca sportiva	oonah jahkkah sporteevah
stockings	delle calze da donna	dayllay kahltsay dah donnah
suit (man's)	un completo	oon koamplaytoa
suit (woman's)	un completo	oon koamplaytoa
suspenders	delle bretelle	dayllay braytehllay
sweater	una giacchetta	oonah jahkkayttah
sweatshirt	una giacca da ginnastica	oonah jahkkah dah jeennarsteekah
T-shirt	una canottiera	oonah kahnoatteeayrah
tennis shoes	delle scarpe da tennis	dayllay skahrpay dah "tennis"
tie	una cravatta	oonah krahvahttah
tights	una calzamaglia	oonah kahltsahmarlyah
top coat	un cappotto	oon kahppoattoa
track suit	un completo per atletica	oon koamplaytoa pair ahtlayteekah
trousers	dei pantaloni	daiee pahntahloanee
underpants (men)	delle mutande da uomo	dayllay mootahnday dah womoa
undershirt	una canottiera	oonah kahnoatteeayrah
vest (Am.)	un panciotto	oon pahnchottoa
vest (Br.)	una camiciola	oonah kahmeecholah
waistcoat	un panciotto	oon pahnchottoa

belt	la cintura	lah cheentoorah
buckle	la fibbia	lah feebbeeah
button	il bottone	eel boattoanay
cuffs	i polsini	ee poalseenee
elastic	l'elastico	laylahsteekoa
pocket	la tasca	lah tarskah
shoe laces	i lacci da scarpe	ee latchee dah skahrpay
zip (zipper)	la cerniera	lah chehrneeayrah

Electrical appliances and accessories—Records

In Italy you will usually find 220-volt current, though some
older buildings, particularly in Rome, have 125-volt outlets.
In Italian-speaking Switzerland the standard voltage is 220
volts. However, plugs have different types of pins and you
may have to get a special adaptor in order to be able to use
your electrical appliances.

What's the voltage?	Qual è il voltaggio?	kwahl ai eel voaltahdjoa
I want a plug for this...	Desidero una spina per questo...	dayzeedayroa oonah speenah pair kooaystoa
Do you have a battery for this?	Ha una pila per questo?	ah oonah peelah pair kooaystoa
This is broken. Can you repair it?	È rotto. Me lo può riparare?	ai roattoa. may loa pwo reepahrarray
When will it be ready?	Quando sarà pronto?	kwahndoa sahrah proantoa
I'd like a/an/some...	Vorrei...	vorraiee
adaptor	una presa multipla	oonah prayzah moolteeplah
amplifier	un amplificatore	oon ahmpleefeekahtoaray
battery	una pila	oonah peelah
blender	un frullatore	oon froollahtoaray
(wall) clock	un orologio (da muro)	oon oaroaloioa (dah mooroa)
food mixer	un mixer	oon "mixer"
hair dryer	un asciugacapelli	oon ashoogahkahpayllee
(travelling) iron	un ferro da stiro (da viaggio)	oon fehrroa dah steeroa (dah veeahdjoa)
kettle	un bollitore	oon boalleetoaray
percolator	una macchinetta per il caffè	oonah mahkkeenehttah pair eel kahffai
plug	una spina	oonah speenah
portable...	...portatile	...poartarteelay
radio	una radio	oonah rardeeoa
car radio	un'autoradio	unowtoarardeeoa
record player	un giradischi	oon jeerahdeeskee
shaver	un rasoio	oon rahssoaeeoa
speakers	degli altoparlanti	daylyee ahltoapahrlahntee
tape recorder	un registratore	oon rayjeestrahtoaray
cassette tape recorder	un registratore a cassette	oon rayjeestrahtoaray ah kasssayttay

television	**un televisore**	oon taylayveezoaray
colour television	**un televisore a colori**	oon taylayveezoaray ah koaloaree
toaster	**un tostapane**	oon toastahparnay
transformer	**un trasformatore**	oon trahsfoarmahtoaray

Record shop

Do you have any records by...?	**Avete dischi di...?**	ahvaytay deeskee dee
Can I listen to this record?	**Posso ascoltare questo disco?**	posssoa ahskoaltarray kooaystoa deeskoa
I'd like a cassette.	**Vorrei una cassetta.**	vorraiee oonah kahsssayttah
I want a new needle.	**Vorrei una puntina nuova.**	vorraiee oonah poonteenah nwawvah

L.P. (33 rpm)	**33 giri**	trayntahtrai jeeree
E.P. (45 rpm)	**super 45 giri**	soopair kwahrahntahcheengkooay jeeree
single	**45 giri**	kwahrahntahcheengkooay jeeree

chamber music	**musica da camera**	moozeekah dah karmayrah
classical music	**musica classica**	moozeekah klahsssseekah
folk music	**musica folcloristica**	moozeekah folkloreesteekah
instrumental music	**musica strumentale**	moozeekah stroomayntarlay
jazz	**jazz**	"jazz"
light music	**musica leggera**	moozeekah laydjairah
orchestral music	**musica sinfonica**	moozeekah seenfoneekah
pop music	**musica pop**	moozeekah pop

Hairdressing—Barber's

I don't speak much Italian.	Non parlo molto l'italiano.	noan pahrloa moaltoa leetahleearnoa
I'm in a hurry.	Ho fretta.	oa frayttah
I want a haircut, please.	Per favore, mi tagli i capelli.	pair fahvoaray mee tarlyee ee kahpayllee
I'd like a shave.	Vorrei che mi radesse.	vorraiee kay mee rahdaysssay
Don't cut it too short.	Non li tagli troppo corti.	noan lee tarlyee troppoa koartee
Scissors only, please.	Solo con le forbici, per favore.	soaloa kon lay foarbee-chee pair fahvoaray
A razor cut, please.	Col rasoio, per favore.	kol rahssoaeeoa pair fah-voaray
Don't use the clippers.	Non usi la macchi-netta.	noan oozee lah mahkkee-nehttah
Just a trim, please.	Solo una spuntatina, per favore.	soaloa oonah spoontah-teenah pair fahvoaray
That's enough off.	Basta così.	bahstah kawssee
A little more off the...	Ancora un po'...	ahngkoarah oon po
back	dietro	deeaytroa
neck	sul collo	sool kolloa
sides	ai lati	ahee lartee
top	in cima	een cheemah
I don't want any cream.	Non voglio della crema.	noan volyoa dayllah kraimah
Would you please trim my...?	Per favore, vuole spuntarmi...?	pair fahvoaray vwawlay spoontahrmee
beard	la barba	lah bahrbah
moustache	i baffi	ee bahffee
sideboards (sideburns)	le basette	lay bahzayttay
Thank you. That's fine.	Grazie. Va bene.	grartseeay. vah bainay
How much do I owe you?	Quanto le devo?	kwahntoa lay dayvoa
This is for you.	Questo è per lei.	kooaystoa ai pair laiee

SHOPPING GUIDE

FOR TIPPING, see page 1

Ladies' hairdressing

SHOPPING GUIDE

Is there a beauty salon in the hotel?	C'è l'istituto di bellezza nell' albergo?	chai leesteetootoa dee behllehttsah nayll-ahlbayrgoa
Can I make an appointment for some-time on Thursday?	Posso avere un appuntamento per giovedì?	posssoa ahvayray oon ahppoontahmayntoa pair joavaydee
I'd like it cut and shaped.	Vorrei il taglio e la messa in piega.	vorraiee eel tarlyoa ay lah maysssah een peeaygah
with a fringe (bangs)	con la frangia	kon lah frahnjah
page-boy style	alla paggio	ahllah pahdjoa
a razor cut	tagliati col rasoio	tahlyartee kol rahssoaeeoa
a re-style	una pettinatura diversa	oonah paytteenahtoorah deevayrsah
with ringlets	a riccioli	ah reetchoalee
with waves	ondulati	oandoolartee
in a bun	a crocchia	ah krokkeeah
I want a...	Voglio...	volyoa
bleach	la decolorazione	lah daykoaloarahtseeoanay
colour rinse	un cachet	oon kahshay
dye	la tintura	lah teentoorah
permanent	la permanente	lah pairmahnayntay
shampoo and set	shampoo e messa in piega	"shampoo" ay maysssah een peeaygah
tint	una sfumatura	oonah sfoomahtoorah
touch up	una ritoccatina	oonah reetoakkahteenah
the same colour	lo stesso colore	loa staysssoa koaloaray
a darker/a lighter colour	un colore più scuro/ più chiaro	oon koaloaray peeoo skooroa/peeoo keearroa
auburn/blond/ brunette	castano/biondo/ bruno	kahstarnoa/beeoandoa/ broonoa
Do you have a colour chart?	Avete una tabella dei colori?	ahvaytay oonah tahbayllah daiee koaloaree
I don't want any hairspray.	Non voglio lacca.	noan volyoa lahkkah
I want a...	Desidero...	dayzeedayroa
manicure	la manicure	lah mahneekoor
pedicure	la pedicure	lah paydeekoor
face-pack	la maschera di bellezza	lah mahskayrah dee behllahttsah

FOR TIPPING, see page 1

Jeweller's—Watchmaker's

Can you repair this watch?	Mi può riparare questo orologio?	mee pwo reepahrarray kooaystoa oaroalojoa
The... is broken.	...è rotto (rotta).	ai roattoa (roattah)
glass/spring	il vetro/la molla	eel vaytroa/lah mollah
strap	il cinturino	eel cheentooreenoa
winder	la chiavetta	lah keeahvehttah
I want this watch cleaned.	Voglio far pulire questo orologio.	volyoa fahr pooleeray kooaystoa oaroalojoa
When will it be ready?	Quando sarà pronto?	kwahndoa sahrah proantoa
Could I please see that?	Mi fa vedere quello, per favore?	mee fah vaydayray kooaylloa pair fahvoaray
I'm just looking around.	Do solo un'occhiata.	daw soaloa oonoakkee-artah
I want a small present for...	Desidero un regalino per...	dayzeedayroa oon raygahleenoa pair
I don't want anything too expensive.	Non voglio qualcosa di troppo caro.	noan volyoa kwahlkawssah dee troppoa karroa
I want something...	Voglio qualcosa...	volyoa kwahlkawssah
better	migliore	meelyoaray
cheaper	più economico	peeoo aykoanawmeekoa
simpler	più semplice	peeoo saympleechay
Do you have anything in gold?	Avete qualcosa in oro?	ahvaytay kwahlkawssah een oroa
Is this real silver?	È argento puro?	ai ahrjayntoa pooroa

If it's made of gold, ask:

How many carats is it?	Quanti carati?	kwahntee kahrartee

When you go to a jeweller's, you've probably got some idea of what you want beforehand. Find out what the article is made of and then look up the name of the article itself in the following lists.

What's it made of?

amber	l'ambra	lahmbrah
amethyst	l'ametista	lahmayteestah
chromium	il cromo	eel kromoa
copper	il rame	eel rarmay
coral	il corallo	eel koarahlloa
crystal	il cristallo	eel kreestahlloa
cut glass	il vetro tagliato	eel vaytroa tahlyartoa
diamond	il diamante	eel deeahmahntay
ebony	l'ebano	laybahnoa
emerald	lo smeraldo	loa smayrahldoa
enamel	lo smalto	loa smahltoa
glass	il vetro	eel vaytroa
gold	l'oro	loroa
gold plate	placcato d'oro	plahkkahtoa doroa
ivory	l'avorio	lahvoreeoa
jade	la giada	lah jardah
onyx	l'onice	loneechay
pearl	la perla	lah pehrlah
pewter	il peltro	eel payltroa
platinum	il platino	eel plarteenoa
ruby	il rubino	eel roobeenoa
sapphire	lo zaffiro	loa dzahffeeroa
silver	l'argento	lahrjayntoa
silver plate	placcato d'argento	plahkkahtoa dahrjayntoa
stainless steel	l'acciaio inossida-bile	lahtchareeoa eenoass-seedahbeelay
topaz	il topazio	eel toapartseeoa
turquoise	il turchese	eel toorkayzay

What is it?

I'd like a/an/some...	Vorrei...	vorraiee
bangle	un braccialetto rigido	oon brahtchahlehttoa reejeedoa
beads	un rosario	oon rawzarreeoa
bracelet	un braccialetto	oon brachtchahlehttoa
charm bracelet	un ciondolo per braccialetto	oon choandoaloa pair brahtchahlehttoa
brooch	una spilla	oonah speellah
cameo	un cammeo	oon kahmmayoa
chain	una catenina	oonah kahtayneenah
charm	un ciondolo	oon choandoaloa
cigarette case	un portasigarette	oon portahsseegahrayttay
cigarette lighter	un accendino	oon ahtchayndeenoa

clip	un fermaglio	oon fayrmarlyoa
clock	un orologio	oon oaroalojoa
alarm clock	una sveglia	oonah svaylyah
travelling-clock	un orologio da viaggio	oon oaroalojoa dah veeahdjoa
collar stud	un bottoncino da colletto	oon boattoancheenoa dah koallayttoa
cross	una croce	oonah kroachay
cuff-links	dei gemelli	daie jaymehllee
cutlery	delle posate	dayllay poassartay
earrings	degli orecchini	daylyee oaraykkeenee
jewel box	un portagioielli	oon portahjoeeehllee
manicure set	un completo per manicure	oon koamplaytoa pair mahneekoor
mechanical pencil	una matita a mina cadente	oonah mahteetah ah meenah kahdayntay
necklace	una collana	oonah koallarnah
pendant	un pendente	oon payndayntay
pin	uno spillo	oonoa speelloa
powder compact	un portacipria	oon portahcheepreeah
propelling pencil	una matita a mina cadente	oonah mahteetah ah meenah kahdayntay
ring	un anello	oon ahnehlloa
engagement ring	un anello di fidanzamento	oon ahnehlloa dee feedahntsahmayntoa
signet ring	un anello con sigillo	oon ahnehlloa kon seejeelloa
wedding ring	una fede nuziale	oonah fayday nootseearlay
rosary	un rosario	oon rawzarreeoa
silverware	dell'argenteria	dayllahrjayntayreeah
snuff box	una tabacchiera	oonah tahbahkkeeayrah
strap	un cinturino	oon cheentooreenoa
chain strap	a catena	ah kahtaynah
leather strap	di pelle	dee pehllay
watch strap	da orologio	dah oaroalojoa
tie clip	un fermacravatte	oon fayrmahkrahvahttay
tie pin	uno spillo per cravatta	oonoa speelloa pair krahvahttah
vanity case	una borsetta per il trucco	oonah boarsehttah pair eel trookkoa
watch	un orologio	oon oaroalojoa
pocket watch	da tasca	dah tahskah
with a second hand	con lancetta per i secondi	kon lahnchehttah pair ee saykoandee
wristwatch	da polso	dah poalsoa

Laundry—Dry cleaning

If your hotel doesn't have its own laundry or dry cleaning service, ask the porter:

Where's the nearest laundry/dry cleaner's?	Dov'è la più vicina lavanderia/tintoria?	doavai lah peeoo vee-cheenah lahvahndayreeah/teentoareeah
I want these clothes...	Voglio far...questi abiti.	volyoa farr...kooaystee arbeetee
cleaned	pulire	pooleeray
pressed	stirare (con la pressa)	steerarray (kon lah prehsssah)
ironed	stirare	steerarray
washed	lavare	lahvarray
When will it be ready?	Quando sarà pronto?	kwahndoa sahrah proantoa
I need it...	Ne ho bisogno...	nay oa beezoañoa
today	oggi	odjee
tonight	stasera	stahssayrah
tomorrow	domani	doamarnee
before Friday	prima di venerdì	preemah dee vaynayrdee
Can you... this?	Mi può... questo?	mee pwo... kooaystoa
mend	rammendare	rahmmayndarray
patch	rappezzare	rappehttsarray
stitch	cucire	koocheeray
Can you sew on this button?	Può attaccare questo bottone?	pwo ahttahkkahray kooaystoa boattoanay
Can you get this stain out?	Mi può togliere questa macchia?	mee pwo tolyayray kooaystah mahkkeeah
Can this be invisibly mended?	Mi può fare un rammendo invisibile?	mee pwo farray oon rahmmayndoa eenveezeebeelay
This isn't mine.	Questo non è mio.	kooaystoa noan ai meeoa
There's one piece missing.	Manca un capo.	mahnkah oon karpoa
There's a hole in this.	C'è un buco in questo.	chai oon bookoa een kooaystoa
Is my laundry ready?	È pronta la mia biancheria?	ai prontah lah meeah beeahngkayreeah

Photography

| I want an inexpensive camera. | Voglio una mao china fotografica economica. | volyoa oonah mahkkeenah foatoagrarfeekah aykoa-nomeekah |
| Show me that one in the window. | Mi faccia vedere quella in vetrina. | mee fahtchah vaydayray kooayllah een vaytreenah |

Film

Film sizes aren't always indicated the same way in Europe as in the U.S. and Great Britain. Listed below you'll find some equivalents and translations which will be useful.

I'd like a...	Vorrei...	vorraiee
cartridge	un rotolo	oon rotoaloa
film for this camera	una pellicola per questa macchina	oonah pehlleekoalah pair kooaystah mahkkeenah
a...film	una pellicola...	oonah pehlleekoalah
120	sei per sei (6×6)	sehee pair sehee
127	quattro per quattro (4×4)	kwahttroa pair kwahttroa
135	ventiquattro per trentasei (24×36)	vaynteekwahttroa pair trayntahssehee
620	seicentoventi	seheechehntoavayntee
8-mm	otto millimetri	ottoa meelleemaytree
super 8	super otto	soopair ottoa
16-mm	sedici millimetri	saydeechee meelleemaytree
20 exposures	venti pose	vayntee poazay
36 exposures	trentasei pose	trayntahssehee poazay
this ASA/DIN number	questo numero ASA/DIN	kooaystoa noomayroa arsah/deen
fast	rapido	rarpeedoa
fine grain	a grana fine	ah grarnah feenay
black and white	bianco e nero	beeahngkoa ay nayroa
colour	a colori	ah koaloaree
colour negative	negativo a colori	naygahteevoa ah koaloaree
colour slide	diapositive a colori	deeahpoazeeteevay ah koaloaree
artificial light type (indoor)	per luce artificiale	pair loochay ahrteefee-charlay
daylight type (outdoor)	per luce naturale	pair loochay nahtoorarlay
Does the price include processing?	Nel prezzo è incluso lo sviluppo?	nayl prehttsoa ai eeng-kloozoa loa sveeslooppoa

SHOPPING GUIDE

FOR NUMBERS, see page 176

Processing

How much do you charge for developing?	**Quanto fate pagare per lo sviluppo?**	kwahntoa fartay pahgarray pair loa sveelooppoa
I want... prints of each negative.	**Voglio...stampe per ogni negativa.**	volyoa... stahmpay pair oañee naygahteevah
with a mat finish	**su carta opaca**	soo kahrtah oaparkah
with a glossy finish	**su carta lucida**	soo kahrtah loocheedah
Will you please enlarge this?	**Mi può ingrandire questo, per favore?**	mee pwo eenggrahndeeray kooaystoa pair fahvoaray
When will it be ready?	**Quando sarà pronto?**	kwahndoa sahrah prontoa

Accessories and repairs

I want a/some...	**Voglio...**	volyoa
flash bulbs/cubes	**delle lampadine/dei cubi per il flash**	dayllay lahmpahdeenay/daiee koobee pair eel "flash"
for black and white	**per bianco e nero**	pair beeahngkoa ay nayroa
for colour	**per foto a colori**	pair foatoa ah koaloaree
filter	**un filtro**	oon feeltroa
red/yellow	**rosso/giallo**	roasssoa/jahlloa
Can you repair this camera?	**Può riparare questa macchina fotografica?**	pwo reepahrarray kooaystah mahkkeenah foatoagrarfeekah
The film is jammed.	**La pellicola è bloccata.**	lah pehlleekoalah ai bloakkartah
There's something wrong with the...	**... è rotto (rotta).**	...ai roattoa (roattah)
exposure counter	**il contatore di esposizioni**	eel koantahtoaray dee ayspoazeetseeoaanee
film winder	**la leva d'avanzamento della pellicola**	lah layvah dahvahntsahmayntoa dayllah pehlleekoalah
flash attachment	**l'attaccatura del flash**	lahttahkkahtoorah dayl "flash"
lens	**l'obiettivo**	loabeeaytteevoa
light meter	**l'esposimetro**	layspoazeemaytroa
rangefinder	**il telemetro**	eel taylaymaytroa
shutter	**l'otturatore**	loattoorahtoaray

Provisions

Here's a basic list of food and drink that you might want on a picnic or for the occasional meal at home:

I'd like a/an/some…, please.	**Per favore, vorrei…**	pair fahvoaray vorraiee
apples	delle mele	dayllay maylay
bananas	delle banane	dayllay bahnarnay
biscuits (Br.)	dei biscotti	daiee beeskoattee
bread	del pane	dayl parnay
butter	del burro	dayl boorroa
cake	un dolce	oon doalchay
candy	dei dolciumi	daiee doalchoomee
cheese	del formaggio	dayl foarmahdjoa
chocolate	della cioccolata	dayllah chokkoalartah
coffee	del caffè	dayl kahffai
cold cuts	degli affettati	daylyee ahffehttartee
cookies	dei biscotti	daiee beeskoattee
cooking fat	del grasso per cucinare	dayl grahsssoa pair koocheenarray
cream	della crema	dayllah kraimah
crisps	delle patatine fritte	dayllay pahtahteenay freettay
cucumbers	dei cetrioli	daiee chaytreeolee
eggs	delle uova	dayllay ooawvvah
flour	della farina	dayllah fahreenah
frankfurters	dei Würstel	daiee "würstel"
ham	del prosciutto	dayl proashoottoa
hamburgers	degli hamburger	daylyee "hamburger"
ice-cream	un gelato	oon jaylartoa
lemons	dei limoni	daiee leemoanee
lettuce	della lattuga	dayllah lahttoogah
luncheon meat	una salsiccia	oonah sahlseetchah
milk	del latte	dayl lahttay
mustard	della senape	dayllah saynahpay
oranges	delle arance	dayllay ahrahnchay
peppers	dei peperoni	daiee paypayroanee
pickles	dei sottaceti	daiee soattahchaytee
potato chips	delle patatine fritte	dayllay pahtahteenay freettay
potatoes	delle patate	dayllay pahtartay
rolls	dei panini	daiee pahneenee
salad	dell'insalata	daylleensahlartah
salami	del salame	dayl sahlarmay
salt	del sale	dayl sarlay

PROVISIONS

sandwiches	**dei sandwich**	**dai**ee "sandwich"
sausages	**delle salsicce**	**day**llay sahl**seet**chay
soft drink	**una bibita**	**oo**nah **bee**beetah
spaghetti	**degli spaghetti**	**day**lyee spah**geht**tee
sugar	**dello zucchero**	**day**lloa **tsook**kayroa
sweets	**dei dolciumi**	**dai**ee doal**choo**mee
tea	**del tè**	dayl tay
tomatoes	**dei pomodoro**	**dai**ee poamoa**daw**roa

And don't forget…

a bottle opener	**un apribottiglia**	oon ahpreebot**teel**yah
a corkscrew	**un cavatappi**	oon kahvah**tahp**pee
matches	**dei fiammiferi**	**dai**ee feeahm**mee**fayree
(paper) napkins	**dei tovaglioli (di carta)**	**dai**ee toavah**lyo**lee (dee **kahr**tah)
a tin (can) opener	**un apriscatole**	oon ahpree**skah**toalay

---

Weights and measures

1 kilogram or kilo (kg) = 1000 grams (g)

100 g = 3.5 oz.	½ kg = 1.1 lb.
200 g = 7.0 oz.	1 kg = 2.2 lb.

1 oz. = 28.35 g
1 lb. = 453.60 g

---

1 litre (l) = 0.88 imp. quarts = 1.06 U.S. quarts

1 imp. quart = 1.14 l	1 U.S. quart = 0.95 l
1 imp. gallon = 4.55 l	1 U.S. gallon = 3.8 l

---

barrel	**un barile**	oon **bar**reelay
box	**una scatola**	**oo**nah **skah**toalah
can	**una lattina**	**oo**nah laht**tee**nah
carton	**una stecca**	**oo**nah **stayk**kah
crate	**una cassa**	**oo**nah **kahs**ssah
jar	**un vaso**	oon **var**zoa
packet	**un sacchetto**	oon sahk**kehtt**oa
tin	**una lattina**	**oo**nah laht**tee**nah
tube	**un tubo**	oon **too**boa

Souvenirs

Italy is particularly noted for its top fashion for both men and women. You'll find numerous smart shops and boutiques in major cities, some of which specialize in custom-made clothing like blouses and shirts. Articles made of silk are of a high quality.

Hand-fashioned jewelry made of amber, gold, silver and tortoise shell as well as cameos are particularly appreciated. Often depending upon the region, you'll come upon fine articles made of leather, olivewood or straw or embroidered clothing and accessories.

antiques	antichità	ahnteekeetah
ceramics	ceramica	chayrarmeekah
doll	bambola	bahmboalah
flask of Chianti	fiasco di Chianti	feearskoa dee keeahntee
glassware	articoli di vetro	ahrteekoalee dee vehtroa
high fashion	alta moda	ahltah modah
jewelry	gioielli	joeeehllee
knitwear	maglieria	mahlyayreeah
leather work	pelletteria	payllayttayreeah
needlework	ricamo	reekarmao
porcelain	porcellana	poarchayllarnah
shoes	scarpe	skahrpay
silk	seta	saitah
toys	giocattoli	joakahttoalee
woodwork	lavoro in legno	lahvoaroa een lehñoa

SOUVENIRS

In Switzerland, you'll find a vast array of watches at prices often well below those at home. An export certificate will save you duty on gold watches or jewelry valued at over 500 francs. The Swiss are also noted for their ceramics, embroidered and handwoven textiles, music boxes and wood carvings.

chocolate	cioccolato	choakkoalartoa
cuckoo clock	orologio a cucù	oaroalojoa ah kookoo
earthen pitcher	boccalino	boakkahleenoa
linen	biancheria	beeahngkayreeah
ski equipment	equipaggiamento da sci	aykooeepahdjahmayntoa dah shee
watch	orologio	oaroalojoa

Tobacconist's

Cigarettes can be bought at the *Sali e Tabacchi* shops, indicated by a sign showing a silver T on a black background.

As at home, cigarettes are generally referred to by their brand names: *Nazionali, Esportazione, Macedonia,* etc. These brands are locally manufactured and quite cheap. Foreign cigarettes are heavily taxed and therefore expensive.

Buying

Give me a/some…, please.	**Per favore, mi dia…**	pair fahvoaray mee deeah
box of…	**una scatola di…**	oonah skahtoalah dee
chewing tobacco	**del tabacco da masticare**	dayl tahbahkkoa dah mahsteekarray
cigar	**un sigaro**	oon seegahroa
cigars	**dei sigari**	daiee seegahree
cigarette case	**un portasigarette**	oon portahsseegahrayttay
cigarette holder	**un bocchino**	oon boakkeenoa
flints	**delle pietrine**	dayllay peeaytreenay
lighter	**un accendino**	oon ahtchayndeenoa
lighter fluid/gas	**della benzina/del gaz per accendino**	dayllah bayndzeenah/ dayl gahz pair ahtchayndeenoa
refill for a lighter	**un ricambio per accendino**	oon reekahmbeeoa pair ahtchayndeenoa
matches	**dei fiammiferi**	daiee feeahmmeefayree
packet of cigarettes	**un pacchetto di sigarette**	oon pahkkayttoa dee seegahrayttay
packet of…	**un pacchetto di…**	oon pahkkayttoa dee
pipe	**una pipa**	oonah peepah
pipe cleaners	**dei nettapipe**	daiee nayttahpeepay
pipe rack	**un portapipe**	oon portahpeepay
pipe tobacco	**del tabacco da pipa**	dayl tahbahkkoa dah peepah
pipe tool	**gli arnesi da pipa**	lyee ahrnayssee dah peepah
snuff	**del tabacco da fiuto**	dayl tahbahkkoa dah feeootoa
tobacco pouch	**una borsa per tabacco**	oonah boarsah pair tahbahkkoa
wick	**uno stoppino**	oonoa stoappeenoa

TOBACCONIST'S

Do you have any...?	**Avete...?**	ahvaytay
American cigarettes	**sigarette americane**	seegahrayttay ahmayree-karnay
English cigarettes	**sigarette inglesi**	seegahrayttay eengglayssee
menthol cigarettes	**sigarette alla menta**	seegahrayttay ahllah mayntah
I'll take two packets.	**Ne prendo due pacchetti.**	nay prehndoa dooay pahkkayttee
I'd like a carton.	**Ne vorrei una stecca.**	nay vorraiee oonah staykkah

filter tipped	**con filtro**	kon feeltroa
without filter	**senza filtro**	sayntsah feeltroa
king-size	**formato lungo**	foarmartoa loonggoa

While we're on the subject of cigarettes, suppose you want to offer somebody one?

Would you like a cigarette?	**Vuole una sigaretta?**	vwawlay oonah seegah-rayttah
Have one of mine.	**Ne prenda una delle mie.**	nay prehndah oonah dayllay meeay
Try one of these.	**Provi una di queste.**	provee oonah dee kooaystay
They're very mild.	**Sono molto leggere.**	soanoa moaltoa laydjayray
They're a bit strong.	**Sono un po' forti.**	soanoa oon po fortee

And if somebody offers you one?

Thank you.	**Grazie.**	grartseeay
No, thanks.	**No, grazie.**	noa grartseeay
I don't smoke.	**Non fumo.**	noan foomoa
I've given it up.	**Ho smesso.**	oa smaysssoa

TOBACCONIST'S

Your money: banks—currency

BANK

Italy's monetary unit is the *lira* (**lee**rah), plural *lire* (**lee**ray), which is actually divided into 100 *centesimi* though you'll never encounter such a petty sum of money.

In Italy, banks are open from 8.30 a.m. to 1.30 p.m. They're closed on Saturdays, Sundays and public holidays. In most important airports and railway stations, banks and currency-exchange offices remain open day and night. Also, the banking hours mentioned here may vary according to the season and the region where you are.

Swiss banks are open from 8 to noon and from 2 to 4 p.m. In the larger cities, you'll find currency-exchange offices *(cambio)* which are open outside the normal hours. The Swiss monetary unit is the *franco* (**frahng**koa), plural *franchi* (**frahng**kee), divided into 100 *centesimi* (chehn**tay**zeemee).

All major credit cards and traveller's cheques are widely accepted.

When you go to a bank, remember to take your passport with you as you may need it.

Where's the nearest bank?	**Dov'è la banca più vicina?**	doavai lah **bahng**kah peeoo veecheenah
Where can I cash a traveller's cheque (check)?	**Dove posso cambiare un traveller's cheque?**	doavay posssoa kahmbeearray oon "traveller's cheque"

Inside

I want to change some dollars.	**Desidero cambiare dei dollari.**	dayzeedayroa kahmbeearray daiee dollahree
I'd like to change some pounds.	**Vorrei cambiare delle sterline.**	vorraiee kahmbeearray dayllay stayrleenay

Here's my passport.	Ecco il mio passaporto.	ehkkoa eel meeoa pahsssahportoa
What's the exchange rate?	Qual è il corso del cambio?	kwahl ai eel koarsoa dayl kahmbeeoa
What rate of commission do you charge?	Quanto trattiene di commissione?	kwahntoa trahtteeaynay dee koammeessseeoanay
Can you cash a personal cheque?	Può cambiare un assegno personale?	pwo kahmbeearray oon ahsssaynoa payrsoanarlay
How long will it take to clear?	Quanto tempo ci vorrà per svincolarlo?	kwahntoa tehmpoa chee voarrah pair sveengkoalahrloa
Can you wire my bank in London?	Può telegrafare alla mia banca a Londra?	pwo taylaygrahfarray ahllah meeah bahngkah ah loandrah
I have...	Ho...	oa
a letter of credit	una lettera di credito	oonah lehttayrah dee kraydeetoa
an introduction from...	una lettera di presentazione di...	oonah lehttayrah dee prayzayntahtseeoanay dee
a credit card	una carta di credito	oonah kahrtah dee kraydeetoa
I'm expecting some money from London. Has it arrived yet?	Aspetto del denaro da Londra. È arrivato?	ahspehttoa dayl daynarroa dah loandrah. ai ahrreevartoa
Please give me... notes (bills) and some small change.	Per favore, mi dia... banconote e della moneta.	pair fahvoaray mee deeah... bahngkoanotay ay dayllah moanaytah
Give me... large notes and the rest in small notes.	Mi dia... in grossi tagli e il resto in piccoli tagli.	mee deeah... een grosssee tahlyee ay eel rehstoa een peekkoalee tahlyee
Could you please check that again?	Può verificare di nuovo questo?	pwo vayreefeekarray dee nwawvoa kooaystoa

Depositing

| I want to credit this to my account. | Desidero accreditare questo sul mio conto. | dayzeedayroa ahkkraydeetarray kooaystoa sool meeoa koantoa |

BANK

| I want to credit this to Mr...'s account. | **Desidero accreditare questo sul conto del signor...** | dayzeedayroa ahkkraydeetarray kooaystoa sool koantoa dayl seeñoar |
| Where should I sign? | **Dove devo firmare?** | doavay dayvoa feermarray |

Currency converter

In a world of fluctuating currencies, we can offer no more than this do-it-yourself chart. You can get a card showing current exchange rates from banks, travel agents and tourist offices. Why not fill in this chart, too, for handy reference?

Italy	£	$
100 lire		
500 lire		
1,000 lire		
10,000 lire		
20,000 lire		
50,000 lire		
100,000 lire		
Switzerland	£	$
50 centesimi		
1 franco		
2 franchi		
5 franchi		
10 franchi		
100 franchi		
500 franchi		
1,000 franchi		

BANK

FOR NUMBERS, see page 176

At the post-office

Post-offices in Italy are open from 8.15 a.m. to 2 p.m. (central post-offices: 8.15 a.m. to 4 p.m.). Swiss post-offices are open from 7.30 to noon and from 1.45 to 6.30 p.m. They're closed on Saturday afternoons in both countries.

Stamps may be obtained from post-offices and tobacconists *(tabaccaio)* in Italy; in Switzerland, from post-offices and automatic stamp dispensers.

Where's the nearest post-office?	**Dov'è l'ufficio postale più vicino?**	doavai looffeechoa poastarlay peeoo veecheenoa
Can you tell me how to get to the post-office?	**Può dirmi come arrivare all'ufficio postale?**	pwo deermee koamay ahrreevarray ahllooffee-choa poastarlay
What time does the post-office open/close?	**A che ora apre/chiude l'ufficio postale?**	ah kay oarah arpray/keeooday looffeechoa poastarlay
What window do I go to for stamps?	**A quale sportello devo rivolgermi per i francobolli?**	ah kwahlay spoartehlloa dayvoa reevoljayrmee pair ee frahngkoaboallee
At which counter can I cash an international money order?	**A quale cassa posso riscuotere un vaglia internazionale?**	ah kwahlay kahsssah poasssoa reeskwotayray oon varlyah eentayr-nahtseeoanarlay
I want some stamps, please.	**Desidero dei franco-bolli, per favore.**	dayzeedayroa daiee frahng-koaboallee pair fahvoaray
I'd like a stamp for this letter/postcard.	**Desidero un franco-bollo per questa lettera/cartolina.**	dayzeedayroa oon frahng-koaboallo pair kooaystah lehttayrah/kahrtoaleenah
What's the postage for a letter to London?	**Qual è l'affranca-tura per una lettera per Londra?**	kwahl ai lahffrahngkahtoo-rah pair oonah lehttayrah pair loandrah
What's the postage for a postcard to Los Angeles?	**Qual è l'affranca-tura per una cartoli-na per Los Angeles?**	kwahl ai lahffrahngkahtoo-rah pair oonah kahrtoa-leenah pair "Los Angeles"
Do all letters go airmail?	**Le lettere vanno per via aerea?**	lay lehttayray vahnnoa pair veeah ahayrayah

POST-OFFICE

I want to send this parcel.	**Vorrei spedire questo pacchetto.**	vorraiee spaydeeray kooaystoa pahkkehttoa
Where's the mailbox?	**Dov'è la cassetta delle lettere?**	doavai lah kahsssehttah dayllay lehttayray
I want to send this by...	**Desidero inviare questo per...**	dayzeedayroa eenveearray kooaystoa pair
airmail	**via aerea**	veeah ahayrayah
express (special delivery)	**espresso**	aysprehsssoa
registered mail	**raccomandata**	rahkkoamahndartah
Where's the poste restante (general delivery)?	**Dov'è lo sportello del fermo posta?**	doavai loa spoartehlloa dayl fayrmoa postah
Is there any mail for me? My name is...	**C'è della posta per me? Mi chiamo...**	chai dayllah postah pair may? mee keearmoa

FRANCOBOLLI	STAMPS
PACCHI	PARCELS
VAGLIA POSTALI	MONEY ORDERS

Telegrams

In Italy and Switzerland, you can either go directly to the post-office to send a telegram or phone it in. Some telegraph offices are open 24 hours a day.

I want to send a telegram May I please have a form?	**Vorrei inviare un telegramma. Può darmi un modulo?**	vorraiee eenveearray oon taylaygrahmmah. pwo darrmee oon modooloa
How much is it per word?	**Quanto costa ogni parola?**	kwahntoa kostah oñee pahrolah
How long will a cable to Boston take?	**Quanto tempo ci vorrà per inviare un telegramma a Boston?**	kwahntoa tehmpoa chee vorrah pair eenveearray oon taylaygrahmmah ah boston
I'd like to reverse the charges.	**Vorrei mandarlo a carico del destinatario.**	vorraiee mahndahrloa ah karreekoa dayl daysteenahtarreeoa

Telephoning

In Italy there are fewer public telephones in the streets than you may be used to. Most people use the public telephone that can be found in cafés and bars. Ask the cashier for tokens (*gettoni*).

Dialling is straightforward and on an inter-city basis (for large towns). You'll find dialling (area) codes in the directory. If you want to make a long-distance call, you'll have to order it in advance.

I'd like a telephone token.	**Vorrei un gettone telefonico.**	vorraiee oon jayttoanay taylayfoneekoa
Where's the telephone?	**Dov'è il telefono?**	doavai eel taylayfoanoa
Where's the nearest telephone booth?	**Dov'è la cabina telefonica più vicina?**	doavai la kahbeenah taylayfoneekah peeoo veecheenah
May I use your phone?	**Posso usare il suo telefono?**	posssoa oozarray eel swoa taylayfoanoa
Do you have a telephone directory for Rome?	**Ha un elenco telefonico di Roma?**	ah oon aylayngkoa taylayfoneekoa dee roamah
Can you help me get this number?	**Mi può aiutare a ottenere questo numero?**	mee pwo ighootarray ah oattaynayray kooaystoa noomayroa

Operator

Do you speak English?	**Parla inglese?**	pahrlah eengglayssay
Good morning, I want Venice 12 34 56.	**Buongiorno. Desidero il 12 34 56 di Venezia.**	bwonjoarnoa. dayzeedayroa eel 12 34 56 dee vaynaitseeah

Note: Numbers are given in pairs.

Can I dial direct?	**Posso chiamare direttamente?**	posssoa keeahmarray deerehttahmayntay
I want to place a personal (person-to-person) call.	**Vorrei fare una telefonata con preavviso.**	vorraiee farray oonah taylayfoanartah kon prayahvveezoa

FOR NUMBERS, see page 176

| I want to reverse the charges. | **Vorrei fare una telefonata con tassa a carico del destinatario.** | vorraiee farray oonah taylayfoanartah kon tahssssah ah karreekoa dayl daysteenahtarreeoa |
| Will you tell me the cost of the call afterwards ? | **Vuol dirmi il costo della telefonata, dopo ?** | vwawl deermee eel kostoa dayllah taylayfoanartah dawpoa |

Telephone alphabet

A	**Ancona**	ahngkoanah	N	**Napoli**	narpoalee
B	**Bari**	barree	O	**Otranto**	oatrahntoa
C	**Catania**	kahtarneeah	P	**Palermo**	pahlehrmoa
D	**Domodossola**	doamoadosssoalah	Q	**cu**	koo
E	**Empoli**	aympoalee	R	**Roma**	roamah
F	**Firenze**	feerehntsay	S	**Sassari**	sarsssahree
G	**Genova**	jainoavah	T	**Torino**	tawreenoa
H	**Hotel**	oatehl	U	**Udine**	oodeenay
I	**Imperia**	eempayreeah	V	**Venezia**	vaynaitseeah
J	**i lunga**	ee loonggah	W	**v doppia**	vee doappeeah
K	**kappa**	kahppah	X	**ix**	eekss
L	**Livorno**	leevoarnoa	Y	**i greca**	ee graykah
M	**Milano**	meelarnoa	Z	**zeta**	dzaitah

Speaking

Hello. This is... speaking.	**Pronto. Qui parla...**	prontoa. kooee pahrlah
I want to speak to...	**Vorrei parlare con...**	vorraiee pahrlarray kon
Would you put me through to... ?	**Mi vuol mettere in comunicazione con... ?**	mee vwawl mayttayray een komooneekahtseeoanay kon
I want extension...	**Mi dia la linea interna...**	mee deeah lah leenayah eentehrnah
Is that... ?	**Parlo con... ?**	pahrloa kon

Bad luck

| Would you please try again later ? | **Per favore, vuol provare di nuovo più tardi ?** | pair fahvoaray vwawl proavarray dee nwawvoa peeoo tahrdee |

Operator, you gave me the wrong number.	**Signorina, mi ha dato il numero sbagliato.**	seeñoareenah mee ah dartoa eel noomayroa zbahlyartoa
Operator, we were cut off.	**Signorina, la comunicazione si è interrotta.**	seeñoareenah lah komooneekahtseeoanay see ai eentehrroattah

Not there

When will he/she be back?	**Quando sarà di ritorno?**	kwahndoa sahrah dee reetoarnoa
Will you tell him/her I called? My name's...	**Vuol dirgli/dirle che ho telefonato? Mi chiamo...**	vwawl deerlyee/deerlay kay oa taylayfoanartoa. mee keearmoa
Would you ask him/her to call me?	**Può chiedergli/chiederle di telefonarmi?**	pwo keeaidayrlyee/keeaidayrlay dee taylayfoanarrmee
Would you please take a message?	**Per favore, può trasmettere un messaggio?**	pair fahvoaray pwo trahzmaytayray oon maysssahdjoa

Charges

What was the cost of that call?	**Quanto è costata la telefonata?**	kwahntoa ai kostartah lah taylayfoanartah
I want to pay for the call.	**Desidero pagare la telefonata.**	dayzeedayroa pahgarray lah taylayfoanartah

C'è una telefonata per lei.	There's a telephone call for you.
Che numero chiama?	What number are you calling?
La linea è occupata.	The line's engaged.
Non risponde.	There's no answer.
Ha chiamato il numero sbagliato.	You've got the wrong number.
Il telefono non funziona.	The phone is out of order.
Egli/Ella è fuori in questo momento.	He's/She's out at the moment.

TELEPHONE

The car

Filling station

We'll start this section by considering your possible needs at a filling station. Most of them don't handle major repairs; but apart from providing you with fuel, they may be helpful in solving alls kinds of minor problems.

Where's the nearest filling (service) station?	**Dove si trova la stazione di rifornimento più vicina?**	doavay see trawvah lah stahtseeoanay dee reeforneemayntoa peeoo veecheenah
I want 20 litres of petrol (gas), please.	**Vorrei 20 litri di benzina, per favore.**	vorraiee 20 leetree dee bayndzeenah pair fahvoaray
I want 30 litres of standard/premium.	**Vorrei 30 litri di normale/super.**	vorraiee 30 leetree dee noarmarlay/soopayr
Give me ... lire worth of petrol (gas).	**Mi dia per ... lire di benzina.**	mee deeah pair ... leeray dee bayndzeenah
Fill her up, please.	**Il pieno, per favore.**	eel peeainoa pair fahvoaray
Please check the oil and water.	**Per favore, controlli l'olio e l'acqua.**	pair fahvoaray koantroallee lawlyoa ay lahkkwah
Give me 2 litres of oil.	**Mi dia 2 litri di olio.**	mee deeah 2 leetree dee awlyoa
Fill up the battery with distilled water.	**Riempia la batteria con acqua distillata.**	reeaympeeah lah bahttayreeah kon ahkkwah deesteellartah
Check the brake fluid.	**Controlli l'olio dei freni.**	koantroallee lawlyoa daiee frehnee

Fluid measures					
litres	imp. gal.	U.S. gal.	litres	imp. gal.	U.S. gal.
5	1.1	1.3	30	6.6	7.8
10	2.2	2.6	35	7.7	9.1
15	3.3	3.9	40	8.8	10.4
20	4.4	5.2	45	9.9	11.7
25	5.5	6.5	50	11.0	13.0

FOR NUMBERS, see page 176

Tire pressure			
lb./sq. in.	kg./cm²	lb./sq. in.	kg./cm²
10	0.7	26	1.8
12	0.8	27	1.9
15	1.1	28	2.0
18	1.3	30	2.1
20	1.4	33	2.3
21	1.5	36	2.5
23	1.6	38	2.7
24	1.7	40	2.8

Would you check the tire pressure?	Può controllare la pressione delle gomme?	pwo koantroallarray lah prayssseeoanay dayllay goammay
1.6 front, 1.8 rear.	1,6 davanti, 1,8 dietro.*	1,6 dahvahntee 1,8 deeehtroa
Please check the spare tire, too.	Per favore, controlli anche la ruota di scorta.	pair fahvoaray koantroallee ahngkay lah rwawtah dee skortah
Can you mend this puncture (fix this flat)?	Può riparare questa foratura?	pwo reepahrarray kooaystah forahtoorah
Would you please change this tire?	Può cambiarmi la gomma, per favore?	pwo kahmbeearrmee lah goammah pair fahvoaray
Would you clean the windscreen (windshield)?	Mi pulisca il parabrezza, per favore.	mee pooleeskah eel pahrahbraydzah pair fahvoaray
Do you have a road map of this district?	Ha una carta stradale della regione?	ah oonah kahrtah strahdarlay dayllah rayjoanay
Where are the toilets?	Dove sono i gabinetti?	doavay soanoa ee gahbeenayttee

* Italians don't say, for instance, one *point* eight but simply one eight or in Italian *uno-otto* (oonoa – ottoa).

Asking the way—Street directions

CAR—INFORMATION

Excuse me.	**Mi scusi.**	mee **skoo**zee
Can you tell me the way to...?	**Può dirmi qual è la strada per...?**	pwo **deer**mee kwahl ai lah **strar**dah pair
How do I get to...?	**Come si va a...?**	**koa**may see vah ah
Where does this road lead to?	**Dove porta questa strada?**	**doa**vay **por**tah **koo**aystah **strar**dah
Are we on the right road for...?	**Siamo sulla strada giusta per...?**	see**ar**moa **sool**lah **strar**dah **joos**tah pair
How far is the next village?	**Quanto dista il prossimo villaggio?**	**kwahn**toa **dees**tah eel **pros**seemoa veel**lahd**joa
How far is it to... from here?	**Quanto dista...da qui?**	**kwahn**toa **dees**tah...dah **koo**ee
Can you tell me, where...is?	**Sa dirmi dov'è...?**	sah **deer**mee doavai
Where can I find this address?	**Dove posso trovare questo indirizzo?**	**doa**vay **pos**soa trawvar-ray koo**ays**toa eendee**reet**tsoa
Where's this?	**Dov'è questo?**	doavai **koo**aystoa

Miles into kilometres										
1 mile = 1.609 kilometres (km.)										
miles	10	20	30	40	50	60	70	80	90	100
km.	16	32	48	64	80	97	113	129	145	161

Kilometres into miles													
1 kilometre (km. = 0.62 miles)													
km.	10	20	30	40	50	60	70	80	90	100	110	120	130
miles	6	12	19	25	31	37	44	50	56	62	68	75	81

Can you show me on the map where I am?	Può indicarmi sulla carta dove mi trovo?	pwo eendeekarrmee soollah kahrtah doavay mee trawvoa
Can you show me on the map where the university is?	Può indicarmi sulla carta dove si trova l'università?	pwo eendeekarrmee soollah kahrtah doavay see trawvah looneevayrseetah
Can I park there?	Posso parcheggiare là?	posssoa pahrkaydjarray lah
Is that a one-way street?	È una strada a senso unico?	ai oonah strardah ah saynsoa ooneekoa
Does the traffic go this way?	La circolazione va in questo senso?	lah cheerkoalahtseeoanay vah een kooaystoa saynsoa

Lei è sulla strada sbagliata.	You're on the wrong road.
Vada diritto.	Go straight ahead.
È laggiù a...	It's down there on the...
sinistra/destra	left/right
Vada fino al primo (secondo) incrocio.	Go to the first (second) crossroads.
Al semaforo, giri a sinistra.	Turn left at the traffic lights.
Giri a destra al prossimo angolo.	Turn right at the next corner.

CAR—INFORMATION

In the rest of this section we'll be more closely concerned with the car itself. We've divided it into two parts:

Part A contains general advice on motoring in Italy and Switzerland. It's essentially for reference and is therefore to be browsed over, preferably in advance.

Part B is concerned with the practical details of accidents and breakdown. It includes a list of car parts and a list of things that may go wrong with them. All you have to do is to show it to the garage mechanic and get him to point to the items required.

Part A

Customs – Documentation

You'll need the following documents when driving in Italy:

passport
international insurance certificate (green card)
registration (log) book
valid driving licence

The nationality plate or sticker must be on the car. Since some countries require a translation of your home driving licence, an international driving permit may save you trouble.

A red warning triangle – for display on the road in case of accident – is compulsory; parking lights are advisable. Crash helmets are mandatory for both riders and passengers on motorcycles and scooters.

Here's my...	Ecco...	ehkkoa
driving licence	**la patente**	lah pahtehntay
green card	**la carta verde**	lah kahrtah vayrday
passport	**il passaporto**	eel pahsssahportoa
registration book	**il libretto di iscrizione**	eel leebrehttoa dee eeskreetseeoanay
I have nothing to declare.	**Non ho nulla da dichiarare.**	noan oa noollah dah deekeeahrarray

CAR—INFORMATION

I've...	Ho...	oa
a carton of cigarettes	una stecca di sigarette	oonah staykkah dee seegahrayttay
a bottle of whisky	una bottiglia di whisky	oonah botteelyah dee "whisky"
a bottle of wine	una bottiglia di vino	oonah botteelyah dee veenoa
We're staying for...	Resteremo...	raystayraymoa
a week	una settimana	oonah saytteemarnah
ten days	dieci giorni	deeaichee joarnee
a fortnight (two weeks)	due settimane	dooay saytteemarnay
a month	un mese	oon maissay

Driving

The classification of roads in Italy is as follows:

Autostrada	Motorway (expressway). Italy has an extensive network of motorways covering the entire country. A toll is charged according to the distance you want to travel. Sign posts indicating the way to a motorway are green.
S.S. 5	*Strada Statale*—first-class main road
S.P. 3	*Strada Provinciale*—second-class through road

The smaller roads, the *strada comunale* for example, vary greatly in quality from region to region.

The traffic regulations valid in Italy and Switzerland are generally the same as those observed in most other European countries. But remember – drive on the right, overtake on the left. Trams have priority over all other vehicles. Unless otherwise indicated, traffic coming from the right always has priority over traffic going straight on.

Horns should be used with moderation, especially at night and near populated areas; however, you'll notice that the Italians themselves don't always seem to have heard about this rule. Outside city limits, it's obligatory to use the direction indicators (turn signals) when overtaking, when changing lanes and when starting from a halt. You may dial 116 from any place in Italy for emergency road assistance.

The police are normally quite lenient with tourists, but don't push your luck too far. For small offences you can be fined on the spot. Here are some phrases which may come in handy in case of confrontation with the *Polizia* or the *Carabinieri*. If you're in serious trouble, insist on an interpreter.

CAR—INFORMATION

I'm sorry, I didn't see the sign.	**Mi dispiace, non ho visto il segnale.**	mee deespeearchay noan oa veestoa eel sayñarlay
The light was green.	**Il semaforo era verde.**	eel saymarfoaroa ayrah vayrday
I'm sorry, I don't speak Italian very well.	**Mi dispiace, non parlo bene l'italiano.**	mee deespeearchay noan pahrloa bainay leetahleearnoa
How much is the fine?	**Quant'è la multa?**	kwahntai lah mooltah

Parking

Use your common sense when parking. Park your vehicle in the direction of moving traffic, not against it. Obey the parking regulations which will be indicated by signs or by lines painted on the kerb (curb).

Excuse me. May I park here?	**Mi scusi, posso parcheggiare qui?**	mee skoozee posssoa pahrkaydjarray kooee
How long can I park here?	**Per quanto tempo posso parcheggiare qui?**	pair kwahntoa tehmpoa posssoa pahrkaydjarray kooee
Do I have to leave my lights on?	**Devo lasciare accese le luci?**	dayvoa lahsharray ahtchayzay lay loochee
Excuse me. Do you have some change for the parking meter?	**Mi scusi, ha la moneta per il parchimetro?**	mee skoozee ah lah moanaytah pair eel pahrkeemaytroa

Road signs

Road signs are practically standardized throughout Western Europe. You should learn to recognize them, particularly those shown on pages 160 and 161.

Listed below are some written signs which you'll certainly encounter when driving in Italy or Switzerland. Obviously, they should be studied in advance. You can't drive and read at the same time!

ACCENDERE I FARI IN GALLERIA	Use headlights before entering tunnel
ACCOSTARE A DESTRA (SINISTRA)	Keep right (left)
ALT	Stop
AREA DI SERVIZIO	Service area
AVANTI	Walk
CADUTA MASSI	Falling rocks
CARABINIERI	Police
CIRCONVALLAZIONE	Ring road (belt highway)
CORSIA D'EMERGENZA	Emergency parking zone
CURVE PER 5 KM.	Bends (curves) for 5 km.
DEVIAZIONE	Diversion/detour
DIVIETO DI SOSTA	No parking
DIVIETO DI SORPASSO	No overtaking (passing)
DOGANA	Customs
LAVORI IN CORSO	Road works ahead (men working)
PAGAMENTO PEDAGGIO	Toll
PARCHEGGIO SOCI A.C.I.	Parking reserved for A.C.I.
PASSAGGIO A LIVELLO	Level (railroad) crossing
PASSAGGIO SCOLARI	School crossing
PERICOLO	Danger
POLIZIA STRADALE	Highway police
RALLENTARE	Reduce speed
SEMAFORI SINCRONIZZATI	Synchronized traffic lights
SENSO UNICO	One way
SILENZIO	Silence
SOCCORSO A.C.I.	A.C.I. emergency road service
SORPASSO	Lane for overtaking (passing)
TRANSITO CON CATENE	Chains required
VICOLO CIECO	Dead end
VIETATO L'ACCESSO	No entry
VIGILI URBANI	City police
ZONA PEDONALE	Pedestrian zone

Part B

Accidents

This section is confined to immediate aid. The legal problems of responsibility and settlement can be taken care of at a later stage.

Your first concern will be for the injured.

CAR—INFORMATION

Is anyone hurt?	**Vi sono dei feriti?**	vee soanoa daiee fayreetee
Don't move.	**Non si muova.**	noan see mwavvvah
It's all right. Don't worry.	**Va tutto bene. Non si preoccupi.**	vah toottoa bainay. noan see prayoakkoopee
Where's the nearest telephone?	**Dov'è il telefono più vicino?**	doavai eel taylayfoanoa peeoo veecheenoa
Can I use your telephone? There's been an accident.	**Posso usare il suo telefono? C'è stato un incidente.**	posssoa oozarray eel swoa taylayfonoa? chai startoa oon eencheedayntay
Call a doctor/an ambulance quickly.	**Chiami un dottore/un'autoambulanza, presto.**	keearmee oon doattoaray/oonowtoaahmboolahntsah prehstoa
There are people injured.	**Ci sono dei feriti.**	chee soanoa daiee fayreetee
Help me get them out of the car.	**Mi aiuti a estrarli dalla macchina.**	mee ighootee ah aystrahrlee dahllah mahkkeenah

Police—Exchange of information

Please call the police.	**Per favore, chiami la polizia.**	pair fahvoaray keearmee lah poaleetseeah
There's been an accident. It's about 2 km. from...	**C'è stato un incidente. È a circa 2 chilometri da...**	chai startoa oon eencheedayntay. ai ah cheerkah 2 keelomaytree dah
I'm on the Florence-Bologna road, 25 km. from Bologna.	**Sono sulla strada Firenze-Bologna, a 25 chilometri da Bologna.**	soanoa soollah strardah feerehntsay-boaloañah ah 25 keelomaytree dah boaloañah
Here's my name and address.	**Ecco il mio nome e indirizzo.**	ehkkoa eel meeoa nomay ay eendeereettsoa

Would you mind acting as a witness?	**Le spiacerebbe fare da testimone?**	lay speeahchayrehbbay farray dah taysteemonay
I'd like an interpreter.	**Vorrei un interprete.**	vorraiee oon eentehrpraytay

Remember to put out a red triangle warning if the car is out of action or impeding traffic.

Breakdown

...and that's what we'll do with this section: break it down into four phases.

1. *On the road*
   You ask where the nearest garage is.

2. *At the garage*
   You tell the mechanic what's wrong.

3. *Finding the trouble*
   He tells you what he thinks is wrong.

4. *Getting it repaired*
   You tell him to repair it and, once that's over, settle the account (or argue about it).

Phase 1—On the road

Where's the nearest garage?	**Dov'è il garage più vicino?**	doavai eel gahrarzh peeoo veecheenoa
Excuse me. My car has broken down. May I use your phone?	**Mi scusi. Ho un guasto all'automobile. Posso usare il suo telefono?**	mee skoozee. oa oon gwarstoa ahllowtoamawbeelay. posssoa oozarray eel swoa taylayfoanoa
What's the telephone number of the nearest garage?	**Qual è il numero di telefono del garage più vicino?**	kwahl ai eel noomayroa dee taylayfoanoa dayl gahrarzh peeoo veecheenoa
I've had a breakdown at...	**Ho avuto un guasto a...**	oa ahvootoa oon gwarstoa ah
We're on the Rome-Naples motorway (expressway), about 10 km. from Naples.	**Siamo sull'autostrada Roma-Napoli a circa 10 chilometri da Napoli.**	seearmoa soollowtoastrardah roamah-narpoalee ah cheerkah 10 keelomaytree dah narpoalee

CAR—REPAIRS

Can you send a mechanic?	Può mandare un meccanico?	pwo mahndarray oon maykkarneekoa
Can you send a truck to tow my car?	Può mandare un autocarro per rimorchiare la mia macchina?	pwo mahndarray oonow-toakahrroa pair reemoar-keearray lah meeah mahkkeenah
How long will you be?	Quanto tempo impiegherete?	kwahntoa tehmpoa eempeeaygayraytay

Phase 2—At the garage

Can you help me?	Può aiutarmi?	pwo ighootarrmee
I don't know what's wrong with it.	Non so dove sia il guasto.	noan soa doavay seeah eel gwarstoa
I think there's something wrong with the...	Penso che...non funzioni (funzionino).	paynsoa kay...noan foontseeoanee (foontsee-oaneenoa)
battery	la batteria	lah bahttayreeah
brakes	i freni	ee frehnee
bulbs	le lampade	lay lahmpahday
carburettor	il carburatore	eel kahrboorahtoaray
clutch	la frizione	lah freetseeoanay
contact	il contatto	eel koantahttoa
cooling system	il sistema di raffreddamento	eel seestehmah dee rahf-frayddahmayntoa
dipswitch (dimmer switch)	il commutatore delle luci	eel koammootahtoaray dayllay loochee
dynamo	la dinamo	lah deenahmoa
electrical system	l'impianto elettrico	leempeeahntoa aylehttreekoa
engine	il motore	eel mawtoaray
exhaust pipe	il tubo di scappamento	eel tooboa dee skahppah-mayntoa
fan	il ventilatore	eel vaynteelahtoaray
filter	il filtro	eel feeltroa
fuel pump	la pompa della benzina	lah poampah dayllah bayndzeenah
fuel tank	il serbatoio della benzina	eel sayrbahtoeeoa dayllah bayndzeenah
gears	le marce	lay mahrchay
generator	il generatore	eel jaynayrahtoaray
hand brake	il freno a mano	eel frehnoa ah marnoa
headlights	i fari anteriori	ee farree ahntayreeoaree
heating	il riscaldamento	eel reeskahldahmayntoa
horn	il clacson	eel klaksoan

CAR—REPAIRS

ignition system	l'accensione	lahtchaynseeoanay
indicator	la freccia di direzione	lah fraytchah dee deeraytseeoanay
lights	le luci	lay loochee
brake	dei freni	daiee frehnee
rear (tail)	posteriori	poastayreeoaree
reversing (back-up)	della retromarcia	dayllah rehtroamahr-chah
lining and covering	la guarnizione e il rivestimento	lah gwahrneetseeoanay ay eel reevaysteemayntoa
lubrication system	il sistema di lubri-ficazione	eel seestehmah dee loo-breefeekahtseeoanay
muffler	la marmitta di scarico	lah mahrmeettah dee skarreekoa
parking brake	il freno a mano	eel frehnoa ah marnoa
radiator	il radiatore	eel rahdeeahtoaray
reflectors	i catarifrangenti	ee kahtahreefrahnjayntee
seat	il sedile	eel saydeelay
silencer	il silenziatore	eel seelayntseeahtoaray
sliding roof	la capote	lah kahpot
sparking plugs	le candele	lay kahndehlay
speedometer	il tachimetro	eel tahkeemaytroa
starter	il motorino d'avvia-mento	eel mawtoareenoa davveeahmayntoa
steering	il volante	eel volahntay
suspension	la sospensione	lah soaspaynseeoanay
(automatic) trans-mission	il cambio (automatico)	eel kahmbeeoa (owtoamarteekoa)
turn signal	la freccia di dire-zione	lah fraytchah dee deeray-tseeoanay
wheels	le ruote	lay rwawtay
wipers	i tergicristalli	ee tayrjeekreestahllee

| RIGHT **DESTRA** (**dehs**trah) | LEFT **SINISTRA** (seeneestrah) | FRONT **DAVANTI** (dah**vahn**tee) | BACK **DIETRO** (deeaitroa) |

It's...	È...	ai
bad	in cattivo stato	een kahtteevoa startoa
blown	strappato	strahppartoa
broken	rotto	roattoa
burnt	bruciato	broochartoa
cracked	incrinato	eengkreenartoa
defective	difettoso	deefehttoassoa

CAR—REPAIRS

disconnected	disinnestato	deezeennehstartoa
dry	secco	saykkoa
frozen	gelato	jaylartoa
jammed	bloccato	blokkartoa
leaking	fessurato	faysssoorartoa
loose	allentato	ahllayntahtoa
misfiring	si accende irrego- larmente	see ahtchaynday eerray- goalahrmayntay
noisy	rumoroso	roomoaroassoa
not working	non funziona	noan foontseeooanah
overheating	surriscaldato	soorreeskahldartoa
short circuiting	un corto-circuito	oon koartoa cheer- kooeetoa
slipping	scivolato	sheevoalartoa
stuck	impigliato	eempeelyartoa
weak	debole	daiboaly
worn	consumato	koansoomartoa

The car won't start.
La macchina non parte.
lah mahkkeenah noan pahrtay

It's locked and the keys are inside.
È chiusa a chiave e le chiavi sono all'interno.
ai keeoossah ah keearvay ay lay keearvee soanoa ahlleentehrnoa

The fan belt is too slack.
La cinghia del ventilatore è troppo lenta.
lah cheenggeeah dayl vaynteelahtoaray ai troppoa lehntah

The radiator is leaking.
Il radiatore perde.
eel rahdeeahtoaray pehrday

I want maintenance and lubrication service.
Desidero il servizio di manutenzione e di lubrificazione.
dayzeedayroa eel sayrvee-tseeoa dee mahnootayn-tseeoanay ay dee loobree-feekahtseeoanay

The clutch engages too quickly.
La frizione stacca troppo in fretta.
lah freetseeoanay stahkkah troppoa een frayttah

The steering wheel's vibrating.
Il volante vibra.
eel volahntay veebrah

The wipers are smearing.
I tergicristalli sono imbrattati.
ee tayrjeekreestahllee soanoa eembrahttartee

The pneumatic suspension is weak.
La sospensione pneumatica è debole.
la soaspaynseeoanay pnayoomarteekah ai daiboalay

The brakes needs adjusting.
I freni devono essere aggiustati.
ee frehnee dayvoanoa ehsssayray ahdjoostartee

Now that you've explained what's wrong, you'll want to know how long it'll take to repair it.

How long will it take to repair?	Quanto tempo ci vorrà per ripararla?	kwahntoa tehmpoa chee vorrah pair reepahrahrlah
How long will it take to find out what's wrong?	Quanto tempo ci vorrà per trovare il guasto?	kwahntoa tehmpoa chee vorrah pair troavarray eel gwarstoa
Suppose I come back in half an hour?	Posso tornare tra mezz'ora?	posssoa toarnarray trah mehddzoarah
Can you give me a lift into town?	Può darmi un passaggio fino in città?	pwo dahrmee oon pahss-sahdjoa feenoa een cheettah

Phase 3—Finding the trouble

It's up to the mechanic either to find the trouble or to repair it. All you have to do is hand him the book and point to the text in Italian below.

Per favore, guardi la seguente lista alfabetica e indichi il pezzo difettoso. Se il cliente vuol sapere perchè non funziona, scelga il termine appropriato dalla lista che segue (è rotto, c'è un corto circuito, ecc.).*

acqua distillata	distilled water
albero	shaft
albero di distribuzione	camshaft
albero motore	crankshaft
ammortizzatore	shock-absorber
aste	stems
basamento	crankcase
batteria	battery
blocco del motore	block
bobina	ignition coil
cambio automatico	automatic transmission
candele	sparking plugs
carburatore	carburettor
cavo	cable
cavi delle candele	sparking-plug leads
cavi dello spinterogeno	distributor leads

* Please look at the following alphabetical list and point to the defective item. If your customer wants to know what's wrong with it, pick the applicable term from the next list (broken, short-circuited, etc.).

cilindro	cylinder
cinghia del ventilatore	fan-belt
collegamento	connection
commutatore delle luci	dipswitch (dimmer switch)
condensatore	condensor
contatto	contact
cremagliera e pignone	rack and pinion
cuscinetto	bearing
cuscinetti di banco	main bearings
denti	teeth
diaframma	diaphragm
dinamo	dynamo (generator)
disco della frizione	clutch plate
elementi della batteria	battery cells
fasce elastiche	piston rings
filtro dell'aria	air filter
filtro della benzina	petrol (gas) filter
filtro dell'olio	oil filter
freno	brake
frizione	clutch
galleggiante	float
generatore	dynamo (generator)
giunto	joint
giunto cardanico	universal joint
guarnizione	lining
guarnizione della testa del cilindro	cylinder head gasket
impianto elettrico	electrical system
indotto del motorino d'avviamento	starter armature
molla della valvola	valve spring
molle	springs
molle a pressione	pressure springs
motore	engine
motorino d'avviamento	starter motor
pattini	shoes
pedale della frizione	clutch pedal
piantone dello sterzo	steering column
pistone	piston
pompa	pump
pompa dell'acqua	water pump
pompa della benzina	petrol pump
pompa d'iniezione	injection pump
pompa dell'olio	oil pump
punteria	tappets
puntine platinate	points

radiatore	radiator
rosette	rings
ruote	wheels
scatola dello sterzo	steering box
sistema di raffreddamento	cooling system
sospensione	suspension
sospensione pneumatica	pneumatic suspension
spazzole	brushes
spinterogeno	distributor
stabilizzatore	stabilizer
sterzo	steering
tamburo del freno	brake drum
termostato	thermostat
testa del cilindro	cylinder head
tiranti trasversali	track rod ends
trasmissione	transmission
valvola	valve
ventilatore	fan

Nella seguente lista troverete le parole per descrivere ciò che non funziona e ciò che deve essere fatto.*

aggiustare	to adjust
allentare	to loosen
allentato	slack
alto	high
avvitare	to grind in
basso	low
batte in testa	knocking
bilanciare	to balance
bloccato	jammed
bruciato	burnt/blown
cambiare	to change
caricare	to charge
consumato	worn
corroso	corroded
corto	short
corto circuito	short-circuited
curvato	warped
debole	weak
difettoso	defective
disinnestato	disconnected
foratura	puncture
gelato	frozen

* The following list contains words which describe what's wrong as well as what may need to be done.

guarnire	to reline
impigliato	stuck
incrinato	cracked
mettere in moto	play
non stacca bene	slipping
perde	leaking
pulire	clean
rapido	quick
rotto	broken
sciolto	loose
secco	dry
si accende irregolarmente	misfiring
si surriscalda	overheating
sostituire	to replace
sporco	dirty
spurgare	to bleed
staccare	to strip down
stringere	to tighten
vibra	vibrating

CAR—REPAIRS

Phase 4—Getting it repaired

Have you found the trouble?	**Ha trovato il guasto?**	ah troavartoa eel **gwar**stoa

Now that you know what's wrong or at least have some idea, you'll want to find out…

Is that serious?	**È grave?**	ai **grar**vay
Can you repair it?	**Può ripararlo?**	pwo reepahrahrloa
Can you do it now?	**Può farlo subito?**	pwo **fahr**loa **soo**beetoa
What's it going to cost?	**Quanto costerà?**	**kwahn**toa kostayrah
Do you have the necessary spare parts?	**Ha i pezzi di ricambio necessari?**	ah ee **peht**tsee dee reekahmbeeoa naychayss-sarree

What if he says "no"?

Why can't you do it?	**Perchè non può farlo?**	pehrkay noan pwo **fahr**loa
Is it essential to have that part?	**È indispensabile avere quel ricambio?**	ai eendeespaynsahbeelay ahvayray kooayl reekahm-beeoa

How long is it going to take to get the spare parts?	Quanto tempo occorre per avere i pezzi di ricambio?	kwahntoa tehmpoa oakkoarray pair ahvayray ee pehttsee dee reekahmbeeoa
Where's the nearest garage that can repair it?	Dov'è il garage più vicino che può riparare il guasto?	doavai eel gahrazh peeoo veecheenoa kay pwo reepahrarray eel gwarstoa
Can you fix it so that I can get as far as...?	Può aggiustarlo in modo che possa andare fino a...?	pwo ahdjoostahrloa een modoa kay posssah ahndarray feenoa ah

If you're really stuck, ask if you can leave the car at the garage. Contact the automobile association or hire another car.

Settling the bill

| Is everything fixed? | Tutto è a posto? | toottoa ai ah poastoa |
| How much do I owe you? | Quanto le devo? | kwahntoa lay dayvoa |

The garage then presents you a bill. If you're satisfied...

Will you take a traveller's cheque?	Accetta un traveller's cheque?	ahtchayttah oon "traveller's cheque"
Thanks very much for your help.	Mille grazie per il suo aiuto.	meellay grartseeay pair eel swoa ighootoa
This is for you.	Questo è per lei.	kooaystoa ai pair laiee

But you may feel that the workmanship is sloppy or that you are paying for work not done. Get the bill itemized. If necessary, get it translated before you pay.

| I'd like to check the bill first. Will you itemize the work done? | Vorrei controllare il conto prima. Vuole specificarmi il lavoro eseguito? | vorraiee koantroallarray eel koantoa preemah. vwolay spaycheefeekahrmee eel lahvoaroa ayzaygooeetoa |

If the garage still won't back down and you're sure you are right, get the help of a third party.

Some international road signs

No vehicles

No entry

No overtaking
(passing)

Oncoming traffic
has priority

Maximum
speed limit

No parking

Caution

Intersection

Dangerous bend
(curve)

Road narrows

Intersection
with secondary
road

Two-way traffic

Dangerous hill

Uneven road

Falling rocks

Give way (yield)

Main road,
thoroughfare

End of restriction

One-way traffic

Traffic goes
this way

Roundabout
(rotary)

Bicycles only

Pedestrians
only

Minimum speed
limit

Keep right
(left if symbol
reversed)

Parking

Hospital

Motorway
(expressway)

Motor vehicles
only

Filling station

No through road

Doctor

Frankly, how much use is a phrase book going to be to you in case of serious injury or illness? The only phrase you need in such an emergency is...

Get a doctor quickly!	**Chiamate un medico, presto!**	keeahmartay oon maideekoa prehstoa

But there are minor aches and pains, ailments and irritations that can upset the best planned trip. Here we can help you and, perhaps, the doctor.

Some doctors will speak English well; others will know enough for your needs. But suppose there's something the doctor can't explain because of language difficulties? We've thought of that. As you'll see, this section has been arranged to enable you and the doctor to communicate. From pages 165 to 171, you find your part of the dialogue on the upper half of each page—the doctor's is on the lower half.

The whole section has been divided into three parts: illness, wounds, nervous tension. Page 171 is concerned with prescriptions and fees.

General

I need a doctor quickly.	**Ho bisogno di un medico, presto.**	oa beezoañoa dee oon maideekoa prehstoa
Can you get me a doctor?	**Può chiamarmi un medico?**	pwo keeahmahrmee oon maideekoa
Is there a doctor here?	**C'è un medico qui?**	chai oon maideekoa kooee
Please telephone for a doctor immediately.	**Telefoni subito a un medico, per favore.**	taylayfoanee soobeetoa ah oon maideekoa pair fahvoaray
Where's there a doctor who speaks English?	**C'è qui un medico che parla inglese?**	chai kooee oon maideekoa kay pahrlah eengglayssay
Where's the surgery (doctor's office)?	**Dov'è l'ambulatorio del medico?**	doavai lahmboolahtoreeoa dayl maideekoa

What are the surgery (office) hours?	**Quali sono le ore di consultazione?**	kwahlee soanoa lay oaray dee koansooltahtseeoanay
Could the doctor come to see me here?	**Il medico può venire a visitarmi qui?**	eel maideekoa pwo vayneeray ah veezeetahrmee kooee
What time can the doctor come?	**Quando può venire il medico?**	kwahndoa pwo vayneeray eel maideekoa

Symptoms

Use this section to tell the doctor what's wrong. Basically, what he'll require to know is:

What? (ache, pain, bruise, etc.)
Where? (arm, stomach, etc.)
How long? (have you had the trouble)

Before you visit the doctor find out the answers to these questions by glancing through the pages that follow. In this way, you'll save time.

Parts of the body

ankle	**la caviglia**	lah kahveelyah
appendix	**l'appendice**	lahppayndeechay
arm	**il braccio**	eel brahtchoa
artery	**l'arteria**	lahrtaireeah
back	**la schiena**	lah skeeainah
bladder	**la vescica urinaria**	lah vaysheekah coreenarreeah
blood	**il sangue**	eel sahnggooay
bone	**l'osso**	losssoa
bowels	**le viscere**	lay veeshayray
breast	**il petto**	eel pehttoa
cheek	**la guancia**	lah gwahnchah
chest	**il torace**	eel toararchay
chin	**il mento**	eel mayntoa
collar-bone	**la clavicola**	lah klahveekoalah
ear	**l'orecchio**	loaraykkeeoa
elbow	**il gomito**	eel goameetoa
eye	**l'occhio**	lokkeeoa
eyes	**gli occhi**	lyee okkee
face	**il viso**	eel veezoa
finger	**il dito della mano**	eel deetoa dayllah marnoa

DOCTOR

DOCTOR

foot	il piede	eel peeayday
forehead	la fronte	lah froantay
gland	la ghiandola	lah geeahndoalah
hair	i capelli	ee kahpayllee
hand	la mano	lah marnoa
head	la testa	lah tehstah
heart	il cuore	eel kworay
heel	il tallone	eel tahlloanay
hip	l'anca	lahngkah
intestines	gli intestini	lyee eentaysteenee
jaw	la mascella	lah mahshehllah
joint	l'articolazione	lahrteekoalahtseeoanay
kidney	il rene	eel rainay
knee	il ginocchio	eel jeenokkeeoa
knee cap	la rotula	lah rotoolah
leg	la gamba	lah gahmbah
lip	il labbro	eel lahbbroa
liver	il fegato	eel faygahtoa
lung	il polmone	eel poalmoanay
mouth	la bocca	lah boakkah
muscle	il muscolo	eel mooskoaloa
neck	il collo	eel kolloa
nerve	il nervo	eel nehrvoa
nervous system	il sistema nervoso	eel seestaimah nehrvoassoa
nose	il naso	eel narssoa
rib	la costola	lah kostoalah
shoulder	la spalla	lah spahllah
skin	la pelle	lah pehllay
spine	la spina dorsale	lah speenah doarsarlay
stomach	lo stomaco	loa stomahkoa
tendon	il tendine	eel tehndeenay
thigh	la coscia	lah koshah
throat	la gola	lah goalah
thumb	il pollice	eel polleechay
toe	il dito del piede	eel deetoa dayl peeayday
tongue	la lingua	lah leenggwah
tonsils	le tonsille	lay toanseellay
urine	l'urina	looreenah
vein	la vena	lah vaynah
wrist	il polso	eel poalsoa

left/on the left side	right/on the right side
sinistro/a sinistra	destro/a destra
(seeneestroa / ah seeneestrah)	(dehstroa / ah dehstrah)

PATIENT

Part 1—Illness

I'm not feeling well.	**Non mi sento bene.**	noan mee sayntoa bainay
I'm ill.	**Mi sento male.**	mee sayntoa marlay
I've got a pain here.	**Ho un dolore qui.**	oa oon doaloaray kooee
His/Her...hurts.	**Ha male al/alla...**	ah marlay ahl/ahllah
I've got (a)	**Ho...**	oa
headache	**il mal di testa**	eel marl dee tehstah
backache	**il mal di schiena**	eel marl dee skeeainah
fever	**la febbre**	lah fehbbray
sore throat	**il mal di gola**	eel marl dee goalah
travel sickness	**il mal di viaggio**	eel marl dee veeahdjoa
I'm constipated.	**Sono costipato.**	soanoa koasteepartoa
I've been vomiting.	**Ho vomitato.**	oa voameetartoa

DOCTOR

1—Indisposizioni

Che disturbo sente?	What's the trouble?
Dove ha male?	Where does it hurt?
Da quanto tempo ha questo dolore?	How long have you had this pain?
Da quanto tempo si sente così?	How long have you been feeling like this?
Tiri su la manica.	Roll up your sleeve.
Si spogli (fino alla vita).	Please undress (to the waist).
Si tolga i pantaloni e le mutande.	Please remove your pants and shorts.

DOCTOR

DOCTOR

PATIENT

I feel...	Mi sento...	mee sayntoa
faint/dizzy	debole/stordito	daiboalay/stoardeetoa
nauseous	la nausea	lah nowsayah
shivery	rabbrividire	rahbbreeveedeeray
I have/She has/ He has (a/an)...	Io ho/Lei ha/ Lui ha...	eeoa oa/layee ah looee ah
abscess	un ascesso	oon ahshehsssoa
asthma	l'asma	lahzmah
boil	un foruncolo	oon foaroongkoaloa
chill	un'infreddatura	ooneenfrayddahtoorah
cold	il raffreddore	eel rahffrayddoaray
constipation	una costipazione	oonah koasteepahtseeoanay
convulsions	le convulsioni	lay koanvoolseeoanee
cramps	i crampi	ee krahmpee
diarrhoea	la diarrea	lah deeahrrayah
fever	la febbre	lah fehbbray
haemorrhoids	le emorroidi	lay aymoarroeedee
hay fever	la febbre del fieno	lah fehbbray dayl feeehnoa
hernia	l'ernia	lehrneeah

DOCTOR

Per favore, si sdrai qui.	Please lie down over here.
Apra la bocca.	Open your mouth.
Respiri profondamente.	Breathe deeply.
Tossisca, per favore.	Cough, please.
Le provo la febbre.	I'll take your temperature.
Le misuro la pressione del sangue.	I'm going to take your blood pressure.
È la prima volta che ha questo disturbo?	Is this the first time you've had this?
Le faccio un'iniezione.	I'll give you an injection.
Desidero un campione dell'urina (delle feci).	I want a specimen of your urine (stools).

PATIENT

indigestion	un'indigestione	ooneendeejaysteeuanay
inflammation of...	un'infiammazione a...	ooneenfeeahmmahtseeoanay ah
influenza	l'influenza	leenflooehntsah
morning sickness	la nausea al mattino	lah nowsayah ahl mahtteenoa
rheumatism	i reumatismi	ee rayoomahteezmee
stiff neck	il torcicollo	eel torcheekolloa
sunburn	una scottatura (di sole)	oonah skottahtoorah (dee soalay)
sunstroke	un colpo di sole	oon koalpoa dee soalay
tonsillitis	la tonsillite	lah toanseelleetay
ulcer	l'ulcera	loolchayrah
whooping cough	la pertosse	lah pairtosssay
It's nothing serious, I hope?	Non è niente di grave, spero.	noan ai neeehntay dee grarvay spayroa
I'd like you to prescribe some medicine for me.	Vorrei che mi prescrivesse delle medicine.	vorraiee kay mee prayskreevaysssay dayllay maydeecheenay

DOCTOR

DOCTOR

Non è nulla di grave.	It's nothing to worry about.
Deve restare a letto per... giorni.	You must stay in bed for... days.
Lei ha...	You've got...
il raffreddore/l'artrite la polmonite/l'influenza un avvelenamento da cibi un'infiammazione a... l'appendicite	a cold/arthritis pneumonia/influenza food poisoning an inflammation of... an appendicitis
Lei fuma/beve troppo.	You're smoking/drinking too much.
Lei è troppo stanco. Ha bisogno di riposo.	You're over-tired. You need a rest.
Voglio che vada all'ospedale per un controllo generale.	I want you to go to the hospital for a general check-up.
Le prescrivo un antibiotico.	I'll prescribe an antibiotic.

PATIENT

I'm a diabetic.	**Ho il diabete.**	oa eel deeah**beh**tay
I've a cardiac condition.	**Sono ammalato di cuore.**	soanoa ahmmah**lar**toa dee **kwo**ray
I had a heart attack in...	**Ho avuto un attacco cardiaco nel...**	oa ahvootoa oon ahttahk-koa kahr**dee**ahkoa nayl
I'm allergic to...	**Sono allergico a...**	soanoa ahl**layr**jeekoa ah
This is my usual medicine.	**Questa è la mia medicina abituale.**	kooaystah ai lah **mee**ah maydee**chee**nah ahbee-**too**arlay
I need this medicine.	**Ho bisogno di questa medicina.**	oa beezoañoa dee kooaystah maydee**chee**nah
I'm expecting a baby.	**Aspetto un bambino.**	ah**spay**ttoa oon bahm-**bee**noa
Can I travel?	**Posso viaggiare?**	poss**soa veeahd**jarray

DOCTOR

Quale dose di insulina ha preso finora?	What dose of insulin are you taking?
Per iniezioni o per via orale?	Injection or oral?
Quale cura sta facendo?	What treatment have you been having?
Che medicine prende attualmente?	What medicine have you been taking?
Ha avuto un (leggero) attacco cardiaco.	You've had a (slight) heart attack.
In Italia non usiamo... Questo è molto simile.	We don't use...in Italy. This is very similar.
Quando deve nascere il bambino?	When's the baby due?
Non può viaggiare fino al...	You can't travel until...

PATIENT

Part 2—Wounds

I've got a/an…. Could you have a look at it?	Ho…Può esaminarmi?	oa…pwo ayzahmeenarrmee
blister	una vescica	oonah vaysheekah
boil	un foruncolo	oon foaroongkoaloa
bruise	una contusione	oonah koantoozeeoanay
burn	una scottatura	oonah skottahtoorah
cut	un taglio	oon tarlyoa
graze	un'escoriazione	oonayskoareeahtseeoanay
insect bite	una puntura d'insetto	oonah poontoorah deensehttoa
lump	un bernoccolo	oon bayrnokkoaloa
rash	un esantema	oon ayzahntehmah
sting	una puntura	oonah poontoorah
swelling	una tumefazione	oonah toomayfahtseeoanay
wound	una ferita	oonah fayreetah
I can't move my… It hurts.	Non posso muovere… Mi fa male.	noan posssoa mwovayray… mee fah marlay

DOCTOR

2—Ferite

(Non) è infetto.	It's (not) infected.
Ha uno spostamento vertebrale.	You've got a slipped disc.
Voglio che faccia una radiografia.	I want you to have an X-ray.
È…	It's…
rotto/slogato	broken/sprained
Ha…	It's…
una lussazione/una lacerazione	dislocated/torn
Ha uno strappo muscolare.	You've pulled a muscle.
Le darò un antisettico.	I'll give you an antiseptic.
Ritorni fra… giorni.	I want you to come and see me in… day's time.

DOCTOR

PATIENT

Part 3—Nervous tension

I'm in a nervous state.	**Sono molto nervoso/nervosa.**	soanoa moaltoa nehrvoassoa/nehrvoassah
I'm feeling depressed.	**Mi sento depresso/ depressa.**	mee sayntoa dayprehsssoa/dayprehsssah
I want some sleeping pills.	**Vorrei dei sonniferi.**	vorraiee daiee soanneefayree
I can't eat.	**Non ho appetito.**	noan oa ahppayteetoa
I can't sleep.	**Non riesco a dormire.**	noan reeehskoa ah doarmeeray
I'm having nightmares.	**Soffro di incubi.**	soaffroa dee eengkoobee
Can you prescribe a...?	**Può prescrivermi...?**	pwo prayskreevayrmee
sedative	**un sedativo**	oon saydahteevoa
tranquilizer	**un tranquillante**	oon trahngkooeellahntay

DOCTOR

DOCTOR

3—Stati ansiosi

Soffre di tensione nervosa.	You're suffering from nervous tension.
Ha bisogno di riposo.	You need a rest.
Quali compresse ha preso?	What pills have you been taking?
Quante al giorno?	How many a day?
Da quanto tempo si sente così?	How long have you been feeling like this?
Le prescrivo delle compresse.	I'll prescribe some pills.
Le prescrivo un sedativo.	I'll give you a sedative.

PATIENT

Prescriptions and dosage

What kind of medicine is this ?	Che genere di medicina è ?	kay jehnayray dee maydeecheenah ai
How many times a day should I take it ?	Quante volte al giorno devo prenderla ?	kwahntay voltay ahl joarnoa dayvoa prehndayrlah
Must I swallow them whole ?	Devo inghiottirle intere ?	dayvoa eenggeeoatteerlay eentayray

Fee

How much do I owe you ?	Quanto le devo ?	kwahntoa lay dayvoa
Do I pay you now or will you send me your bill ?	Pago subito o mi manda la nota ?	pargoa soobeetoa oa mee mahndah lah notah
Thanks for your help, Doctor.	Grazie mille, dottore.	grahtseeay meellay doattoaray

DOCTOR

Ricette e dosi

Prenda...cucchiaini da tè di questa medicina ogni...ore.	Take...teaspoons of this medicine every...hours.
Prenda...compresse con un bicchiere d'acqua...	Take...pills with a glass of water...
...volte al giorno	...times a day
prima dei pasti	before each meal
dopo i pasti	after each meal
fra un pasto e l'altro	between meals
al mattino	in the morning
alla sera	at night

L'onorario

Sono....per favore.	That's...,please.
Paghi ora, per favore.	Please pay me now.
Le manderò il conto.	I'll send you a bill.

FOR NUMBERS, see page 176

DOCTOR

Dentist

Can you recommend a good dentist?	**Può consigliarmi un buon dentista?**	pwo koanseelyarmee oon bwawn daynteestah
Can I make an (urgent) appointment to see Dr....?	**Desidero un appuntamento (urgente) con il dottor...**	dayzeedayroa oon ahppoontahmayntoa (oorjehntay) kon eel doattoar
Can't you possibly make it earlier than that?	**Non è possibile prima?**	noan ai poassseebeelay preemah
I've a toothache.	**Ho mal di denti.**	oa marl dee dehntee
I've an abscess.	**Ho un ascesso.**	oa oon ahshehsssoa
This tooth hurts.	**Mi fa male questo dente.**	mee fah marlay kooaystoa dehntay
at the top	**in alto**	een ahltoa
at the bottom	**in basso**	een bahsssoa
in the front	**davanti**	dahvahntee
at the back	**dietro**	deeehtroa
Can you fix it temporarily?	**Può curarlo provvisoriamente?**	pwo koorarrloa proavveezoareeahmayntay
I don't want it extracted.	**Non voglio un'estrazione.**	noan volyoa oonaystrahtseeoanay
I've lost a filling.	**L'otturazione si è staccata.**	loattoorahtseeoanay see ai stahkkartah
The gum...	**La gengiva...**	lah jaynjeevah
is very sore	**è molto infiammata**	ai moaltoa eenfeeahmartah
is bleeding	**sanguina**	sahnggooeenah

Dentures

I've broken this denture.	**Ho rotto questa dentiera.**	oa roattoa kooaystah daynteeehrah
Can you repair this denture?	**Può ripararmi questa dentiera?**	pwo reepahrarrmee kooaystah daynteeehrah
When will it be ready?	**Quando sarà pronta?**	kwahndoa sahrah proantah

Optician

I've broken my glasses.	**Ho rotto gli occhiali.**	oa roattoa lyoo okkeearlee
Can you repair them for me?	**Può ripararmeli?**	pwo reepahrarrmaylee
When will they be ready?	**Quando saranno pronti?**	kwahndoa sahrahnnoa proantee
Can you change the lenses?	**Può cambiare le lenti?**	pwo kahmbeearray lay lehntee
I want tinted lenses.	**Desidero delle lenti colorate.**	dayzeedayroa dayllay lehntee koaloarartay
I want contact lenses.	**Desidero delle lenti a contatto.**	dayzeedayroa dayllay lehntee ah koantahttoa
I've lost one of my contact lenses.	**Ho perso le lenti a contatto.**	oa pehrsoa lay lehntee ah koantahttoa
Could you give me another one?	**Può darmene un'altra?**	pwo darrmehneh oonahltrah
Have you any contact lens liquid?	**Avete del liquido per lenti a contatto?**	ahvaytay dayl leekooeedoa pair lehntee ah koantahttoa
A large/small bottle, please.	**Un flacone grande/ piccolo, per favore.**	oon flahkoanay grahnday/ peekkoaloa pair fahvoaray
I'd like to buy a pair of binoculars.	**Vorrei acquistare un binocolo.**	vorraiee akkooeestarray oon beenokoaloa
I'd like to buy a pair of sun-glasses.	**Vorrei degli occhiali da sole.**	vorraiee daylyee okkeearlee dah soalay
How much do I owe you?	**Quanto le devo?**	kwahntoa lay dayvoa
Do I pay you now or will you send me your bill?	**Pago subito o mi manda la fattura?**	pargoa soobeetoa oa mee mahndah lah fahttoorah

OPTICIAN

FOR NUMBERS, see page 176

Reference section

Where do you come from?

This page will help you to explain where you're from, where you've been, and where you're going.

Africa	**Africa**	arfreekah
Algeria	**Algeria**	ahljayreeah
Asia	**Asia**	arzeeah
Australia	**Australia**	owstrarlyah
Austria	**Austria**	owstreeah
Belgium	**Belgio**	behljoa
Canada	**Canada**	kahnahdah
China	**Cina**	cheenah
England	← **Inghilterra** ←	eenggeeltehrrah
Europe	**Europa**	ayooropah
France	**Francia**	frahnchah
Germany	**Germania**	jayrmarneeah
Great Britain	**Gran Bretagna**	grahn braytarñah
Greece	**Grecia**	graichah
Holland	**Olanda**	olahndah
Ireland	**Irlanda**	eerlahndah
Israel	**Israele**	eesrahaylay
Italy	**Italia**	eetarlyah
Japan	**Giappone**	jahpponay
Malta	**Malta**	mahltah
Morocco	**Marocco**	mahrokkoa
New Zealand	**Nuova Zelanda**	nwavvvah tsaylahndah
North America	**America del Nord**	ahmaireekah dayl nord
San Marino	**San Marino**	sahn mahreenoa
Scandinavia	**Scandinavia**	skahndeenarveeah
Scotland	**Scozia**	skotseeah
Sicily	**Sicilia**	seecheelyah
South Africa	**Africa del Sud**	arfreekah dayl sood
South America	**America del Sud**	ahmaireekah dayl sood
Soviet Union	**Unione Sovietica**	ooneeoanay soaveeehteekah
Spain	**Spagna**	sparñah
Switzerland	**Svizzera**	sveettsayrah
Tunisia	**Tunisia**	tooneezeeah
United States	**Stati Uniti**	startee ooneetee
Vatican City	**Città del Vaticano**	cheettah dayl vahteekarnoa
Wales	**Galles**	gahllayss
Yugoslavia	**Jugoslavia**	eeoogoaslarveeah

Numbers

0	zero	dzehroa
1	uno	oonoa
2	due	dooay
3	tre	tray
4	quattro	kwahttroa
5	cinque	cheengkooay
6	sei	sehee
7	sette	sehttay
8	otto	ottoa
9	nove	nawvay
10	dieci	deeaichee
11	undici	oondeechee
12	dodici	doadeechee
13	tredici	traydeechee
14	quattordici	kwahttordeechee
15	quindici	kooeendeechee
16	sedici	saydeechee
17	diciassette	deechahssssehttay
18	diciotto	deechottao
19	diciannove	deechahnnawvay
20	venti	vayntee
21	ventuno	vayntoonoa
22	ventidue	vaynteedooay
23	ventitre	vaynteetray
24	ventiquattro	vaynteekwahttroa
25	venticinque	vaynteecheengkooay
26	ventisei	vaynteessehee
27	ventisette	vaynteessehttay
28	ventotto	vayntottoa
29	ventinove	vaynteenawvay
30	trenta	trayntah
31	trentuno	trayntoonoa
32	trentadue	trayntahdooay
33	trentatre	trayntatray
40	quaranta	kwahrahntah
41	quarantuno	kwahrahntoonoa
42	quarantadue	kwahrahntahdooay
43	quarantatre	kwahrahntahtray
50	cinquanta	cheengkwahntah
51	cinquantuno	cheengkwahntoonoa
52	cinquantadue	cheengkwahntahdooay
53	cinquantatre	cheengkwahntahtray
60	sessanta	saysssahntah
61	sessantuno	saysssahntoonoa

02	sessantadue	saysssahntahdooay
63	sessantatre	saysssahntahtray
70	settanta	sayttahntah
71	settantuno	sayttahntoonoa
72	settantadue	sayttahntahdooay
73	settantatre	sayttahntahtray
80	ottanta	oattahntah
81	ottantuno	ottahntoonoa
82	ottantadue	ottahntahdooay
83	ottantatre	ottahntahtray
90	novanta	noavahntah
91	novantuno	noavahntoonoa
92	novantadue	noavahntahdooay
93	novantatre	noavahntahtray
100	cento	chehntoa
101	centouno	chehntoaoonoa
102	centodue	chehntoadooay
110	centodieci	chehntoadeeaichee
120	centoventi	chehntoavayntee
130	centotrenta	chehntoatrayntah
140	centoquaranta	chehntoakwahrahntah
150	centocinquanta	chehntoacheengkwahntah
160	centosessanta	chehntoassaysssahntah
170	centosettanta	chehntoassayttahntah
180	centottanta	chehntottahntah
190	centonovanta	chehntoanoavahntah
200	duecento	dooaychehntoa
300	trecento	traychehntoa
400	quattrocento	kwahttroachehntoa
500	cinquecento	cheengkooaychehntoa
600	seicento	sayeechehntoa
700	settecento	sehttaychehntoa
800	ottocento	ottochehntoa
900	novecento	noavaychehntoa
1000	mille	meellay
1100	millecento	meellaychehntoa
1200	milleduecento	meellaydooaychehntoa
2000	duemila	dooaymeelah
5000	cinquemila	cheengkooaymeelah
10,000	diecimila	deeaicheemeelah
50,000	cinquantamila	cheengkwahntahmeelah
100,000	centomila	chehntoameelah
1,000,000	un milione	oon meelyoanay
1,000,000,000	un miliardo	oon meelyarrdoa

first	**primo**	preemoa
second	**secondo**	saykoandoa
third	**terzo**	tehrtsoa
fourth	**quarto**	kwarrtoa
fifth	**quinto**	kooeentoa
sixth	**sesto**	sehstoa
seventh	**settimo**	sehtteemoa
eighth	**ottavo**	ottarvoa
ninth	**nono**	nonoa
tenth	**decimo**	dehcheemoa
once	**una volta**	oonah voltah
twice	**due volte**	dooay voltay
three times	**tre volte**	tray voltay
a half	**un mezzo**	oon mehddzoa
half a...	**mezzo...**	mehddzoa
half of...	**metà di...**	maytah dee
half (adj)	**mezzo**	mehddzoa
a quarter	**un quarto**	oon kwarrtoa
one third	**un terzo**	oon tehrtsoa
a pair of	**un paio di**	oon pareeoa dee
a dozen	**una dozzina**	oonah doaddzeenah

1982	**millenovecentottantadue** (meellay-noavaychehnt-ottahntahdooay)
1983	**millenovecentottantatre** (meellay-noavaychehnt-ottahntahtray)
1984	**millenovecentottantaquattro** (meellay-noavaychehnt-ottahntahkwahttroa)
1985	**millenovecentottantacinque** (meellay-noavaychehnt-ottahntahcheengkooay)

Time

le dodici
e un quarto
(lay **doa**deechee ay oon
kwahrtoa)

l'una e venti
(loonah ay vayntee)

le due
e venticinque
(lay **doo**ay ay
vaynteecheengkooay)

le tre e mezzo
(lay tray ay mehddzoa)

le quattro
e trentacinque
(lay kwahttroa
ay trayntahcheengkooay)

le cinque
e quaranta
(lay cheengkooay
ay kwahrahntah)

le sette
meno un quarto
(lay sehttay mainoa oon
kwahrtoa)

le otto meno dieci
(lay ottoa mainoa
deeaichee)

le nove
meno cinque
(lay nawvay mainoa
cheengkooay)

le dieci
(lay deeaichee)

le undici e cinque
(lay oondeechee ay
cheengkooay)

le dodici e dieci
(lay **doa**deechee ay
deeaichee)

What time is it?

What time is it?	**Che ore sono?**	kay oaray soanao
It's one o'clock.	**È l'una.**	ai loonah
It's three o'clock.	**Sono le tre.**	soanoa lay tray
Excuse me Can you tell me the time?	**Scusi, può dirmi l'ora?**	skoozee pwo deermee loarah
I'll meet you at... tomorrow.	**Ci incontreremo domani alle...**	chee eengkontrayraymoa doamarnee ahllay
I'm sorry I'm late.	**Mi dispiace, sono in ritardo.**	mee deespeearchay soanoa een reetahrdoa
At what time does... open?	**A che ora apre...?**	ah kay oarah arpray
At what time does... close?	**A che ora chiude...?**	ah kay oarah keeoooday
At what time should I be there?	**A che ora devo venire?**	ah kay oarah dayvoa vayneeray
At what time will you be there?	**A che ora verrete?**	ah kay oarah vayrraytay
Can I come...?	**Posso venire...?**	posssoa vayneeray
at 8 o'clock/at 2:30	**alle 8/alle 2 e mezzo***	ahllay ottoa/ahllay dooay ay mehddzoa
after (prep.)	**dopo**	dawpoa
afterwards	**dopo**	dawpoa
before	**prima**	preemah
early	**presto**	prehstoa
in time	**in tempo**	een tehmpoa
late	**tardi**	tahrdee
midnight	**mezzanotte**	mehddzahnottay
noon	**mezzogiorno**	mehddzoajoarnoa
hour	**ora**	oarah
minute	**minuto**	meenootoa
second	**secondo**	saykoandoa
quarter of an hour	**quarto d'ora**	kwahrtoa doarah
half an hour	**mezz'ora**	mehddzoarah

---

* In ordinary conversation, time is expressed as shown here (see also page 179). However, official time uses a 24-hour clock which means that after noon hours are counted from 13 to 24. For instance, 13.15 would be 1.15 p.m. for us and 20h.30 is 8.30 p.m. At midnight time returns to 0 so that 12.17 a.m. is written 0h.17.

Days

What day is it today?	**Che giorno è oggi?**	kay joarnao ai odjee
Sunday	**domenica**	doamayneekah
Monday	**lunedì**	loonaydee
Tuesday	**martedì**	mahrtaydee
Wednesday	**mercoledì**	mehrkoalaydee
Thursday	**giovedì**	joavaydee
Friday	**venerdì**	vaynayrdee
Saturday	**sabato**	sarbahtoa
in the morning	**al mattino**	ahl mahtteenoa
during the day	**durante il giorno**	doorahntay eel joarnoa
in the afternoon	**nel pomeriggio**	nayl poamayreedjoa
in the evening	**alla sera**	ahllah sayrah
at night	**la notte**	lah nottay
yesterday	**ieri**	eeairee
today	**oggi**	odjee
tomorrow	**domani**	doamarnee
the day before	**il giorno prima**	eel joarnoa preemah
the next day	**il giorno seguente**	eel joarnoa saygooayntay
two days ago	**due giorni fa**	dooay joarnee fah
in three days' time	**in tre giorni**	een tray joarnee
last week	**la settimana scorsa**	lah saytteemarnah skoarsah
next week	**la settimana prossima**	lah saytteemarnah prossseemah
for a fortnight (two weeks)	**per due settimane**	pair dooay saytteemarnay
birthday	**il compleanno**	eel koamplayahnnoa
day	**il giorno**	eel joarnoa
day off	**il giorno di riposo**	eel joarnoa dee reepossoa
holiday	**il giorno festivo**	eel joarnoa faysteevoa
holidays	**le vacanze**	lay vahkahntsay
month	**il mese**	eel maissay
school holidays	**le vacanze scolastiche**	lay vahkahntsay skolarsteekay
vacation	**le vacanze**	lay vahkahntsay
week	**la settimana**	lah saytteemarnah
weekday	**il giorno della settimana**	eel joarnoa dayllah saytteemarnah
weekend	**il fine settimana**	eel feenay saytteemarnah
working day	**il giorno feriale**	eel joarnoa fayreearlay

Note: The names of days and months are not capitalized in Italian.

Months

January	gennaio	jainnighoa
February	febbraio	fehbbrighoa
March	marzo	mahrtsoa
April	aprile	ahpreelay
May	maggio	mahdjoa
June	giugno	jooñoa
July	luglio	loolyoa
August	agosto	ahgoastoa
September	settembre	sayttehmbray
October	ottobre	oattoabray
November	novembre	noavehmbray
December	dicembre	deechehmbray

since June	da giugno	dah jooñoa
during the month of August	durante il mese di agosto	doorahntay eel maissay dee ahgoastoa
last month	il mese scorso	eel maissay skoarsoa
next month	il mese prossimo	eel maissay prossseemoa
the month before	il mese prima	eel maissay preemah
the next month	il mese dopo	eel maissay dawpoa
July 1	il primo luglio	eel preemoa loolyoa
March 17	il diciassette marzo	eel deechahssssehttay mahrtsoa

Letter headings are written thus:

Rome, August 17, 19..	**Roma, 17 agosto 19..**
Milan, Juli 1, 19..	**Milano 1 luglio 19..**

Seasons

spring	la primavera	lah preemahvayrah
summer	l'estate	laystartay
autumn	l'autunno	lowtoonnoa
winter	l'inverno	leenvehrnoa

in spring	in primavera	een preemahvayrah
during the summer	durante l'estate	doorahntay laystartay
in autumn	in autunno	een owtoonnoa
during the winter	durante l'inverno	doorahntay leenvehrnoa

Public holidays

Holidays vary from one region to the other. But only those days are noted below that are national holidays, when all schools, banks, stores, factories and offices are closed. (I = Italy, CH = Switzerland.)

January 1	Primo dell'Anno	New Year's Day	I CH
January 2			CH*
April 25	Anniversario della Liberazione (1945)	Liberation Day	I
May 1	Festa del Lavoro	Labour Day	I
August 15	Assunzione di M.V. (Ferragosto)	Assumption Day	I
November 1	Tutti i Santi	All Saints' Day	I
December 8	Immacolata Concezione	Immaculate Conception	I
December 25	Natale	Christmas Day	I CH
December 26	S. Stefano	St. Stephen	I CH*
Movable dates:	Lunedì di Pasqua (Pasquetta)	Easter Monday	I CH
	Ascensione di N. S.	Ascension Thursday	I CH
	Venerdì Santo	Good Friday	CH*
	Lunedì di Pentecoste	Whit Monday	CH

Seasonal temperatures

Here are the average monthly temperatures in centigrade and Fahrenheit for some Italian cities:

	Milan	Rome	Palermo
January	6 °C (43 °F)	9 °C (48 °F)	13 °C (57 °F)
April	19 °C (66 °F)	19 °C (66 °F)	20 °C (68 °F)
July	24 °C (75 °F)	25 °C (77 °F)	26 °C (79 °F)
October	17 °C (63 °F)	21 °C (70 °F)	22 °C (72 °F)

---

* Most cantons

REFERENCE SECTION

Abbreviations

a.	**arrivo**	arrival
a.C.	**avanti Cristo**	B.C.
A.C.I.	**Automobile Club d'Italia**	Automobile Association of Italy
A.C.S.	**Automobile Club Svizzero**	Automobile Association of Switzerland
a.D.	**anno Domini**	A.D.
A.G.I.P.	**Azienda Generale Italiana Petroli**	Italian Petroleum Company
alt.	**altitudine**	altitude
ca	**circa**	approximately
C.I.T.	**Compagnia Italiana Turismo**	Italian Travel Agency
C.P.	**casella postale**	post office box
C.so	**corso**	avenue
d.C.	**dopo Cristo**	A.D.
ecc.	**eccetera**	etc.
EE	**Escursionisti Esteri**	car number plates for foreigners
E.N.I.T.	**Ente Nazionale Italiano per il Turismo**	National Tourist Organization
F.F.S.	**Ferrovie Federali Svizzere**	Swiss Federal Railways
F.S.	**Ferrovie dello Stato**	National Railways
I.V.A.	**Imposta sul Valore Aggiunto**	value added tax (sales tax)
Mil.	**militare**	military
p.	**partenza**	departure
P.T.	**Poste & Telecomunicazioni**	Post & Telecommunications
P.za	**piazza**	square
R.A.I.	**Radio Audizioni Italiane**	Italian Broadcasting Company
Rep.	**Repubblica**	republic
sec.	**secolo**	century
Sig.	**Signor**	Mr.
Sig.na	**Signorina**	Miss
Sig.ra	**Signora**	Mrs.
s.p.a.	**società per azioni**	Ltd., Inc.
S.P.Q.R.	**Senatus Populusque Romanus**	The Senate and the People of Rome (Latin)
T.C.I.	**Touring Club Italiano**	Italian Touring Association
T.C.S.	**Touring Club Svizzero**	Swiss Touring Association
V.le	**viale**	avenue
V.U.	**Vigili Urbani**	city police

Conversion tables

Centimetres and inches

To change centimetres into inches, multiply by .39.

To change inches into centimetres, multiply by 2.54.

	in.	feet	yards
1 mm	0,039	0,003	0,001
1 cm	0,39	0,03	0,01
1 dm	3,94	0,32	0,10
1 m	39,40	3,28	1,09

	mm	cm	m
1 in.	25,4	2,54	0,025
1 ft.	304,8	30,48	0,304
1 yd.	914,4	91,44	0,914

(32 metres = 35 yards)

Temperature

To convert Centigrade into degrees Fahrenheit, multiply Centigrade by 1.8 and add 32.

To convert degrees Fahrenheit into Centigrade, subtract 32 from Fahrenheit and divide by 1.8.

Metres and feet

The figure in the middle stands for both metres and feet, e.g.,
1 metre = 3.28 feet and 1 foot = 0.30 m.

Metres		Feet
0.30	1	3.281
0.61	2	6.563
0.91	3	9.843
1.22	4	13.124
1.52	5	16.403
1.83	6	19.686
2.13	7	22.967
2.44	8	26.248
2.74	9	29.529
3.05	10	32.810
3.35	11	36.091
3.66	12	39.372
3.96	13	42.635
4.27	14	45.934
4.57	15	49.215
4.88	16	52.496
5.18	17	55.777
5.49	18	59.058
5.79	19	62.339
6.10	20	65.620
7.62	25	82.023
15.24	50	164.046
22.86	75	246.069
30.48	100	328.092

Other conversion charts

For	see page
Clothing sizes	115
Currency converter	136
Distance (miles—kilometres)	144
Fluid measures	142
Tire pressure	143

REFERENCE SECTION

Weight conversion

The figure in the middle stands for both kilograms and pounds, e.g., 1 kilogram = 2.20 pounds and 1 pound = 0.45 kilograms.

Kilograms (kg.)		Avoirdupois pounds
0.45	1	2.205
0.90	2	4.405
1.35	3	6.614
1.80	4	8.818
2.25	5	11.023
2.70	6	13.227
3.15	7	15.432
3.60	8	17.636
4.05	9	19.840
4.50	10	22.045
6.75	15	33.068
9.00	20	44.889
11.25	25	55.113
22.50	50	110.225
33.75	75	165.338
45.00	100	220.450

REFERENCE SECTION

NORTH
NORD
(nord)

WEST
OVEST
(ovehst)

EAST
EST
(ehst)

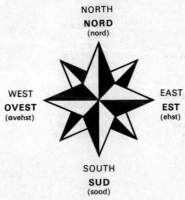

SOUTH
SUD
(sood)

What does that sign mean ?

You're sure to encounter some of these signs or notices on your trip.

Ascensore	Lift (elevator)
Attenti al cane	Beware of the dog
Caldo	Hot
Cassiere	Cashier's
Chiudo	Closed
Da affittare	To let, for hire
Entrare senza bussare	Enter without knocking
Entrata	Entrance
Entrata libera	Free entrance
Freddo	Cold
I trasgressori saranno puniti a norma di legge	Trespassers will be prosecuted
Informazioni	Information
In vendita	For sale
Libero	Vacant
Occupato	Occupied
Pericolo	Danger
Pericolo di morte	Danger of death
Pista per ciclisti	Path for cyclists
Privato	Private
Prudenza	Caution
Riservato	Reserved
Saldi	Sales
Signore	Ladies
Signori	Gentlemen
Spingere	Push
Strada privata	Private road
Suonare, per favore	Please ring
Svendita	Sales
Tirare	Pull
Uscita	Exit
Uscita di emergenza	Emergency exit
Vietato...	...forbidden
Vietato fumare	No smoking
Vietato l'ingresso	No entrance
Vietato toccare	Do not touch

Emergency

By the time the emergency is upon you it's too late to turn to this page to find the Italian for "I'll scream if you…". So have a look at this short list beforehand—and, if you want to be on the safe side, learn the expressions shown in capitals.

Be quick	**Faccia presto**	fahtchah prehstoa
Call the police	**Chiami la polizia**	keearmee la poaleetseeah
CAREFUL	**ATTENTO**	ahttehntoa
Come here	**Venga qui**	vaynggah kooee
Come in	**Entri**	ayntree
Danger	**Pericolo**	payreekoaloa
Fire	**Fuoco**	fwawkoa
Gas	**Gas**	gaz
Get a doctor	**Chiami un medico**	keearmee oon maideekoa
Go away	**Se ne vada**	say nay vardah
HELP	**AIUTO**	ighootoa
Get help quickly	**Chiami dei soccorsi, presto**	keearmee daiee soakkoarsee prehstoa
I'm ill	**Mi sento male**	mee sayntoa marlay
I'm lost	**Mi sono perso**	mee soanoa pehrsoa
I've lost my…	**Ho perso…**	oa pehrsoa
Keep your hands to yourself	**Tenga le mani a posto**	taynggah lay marnee ah poastoa
Leave me alone	**Mi lasci in pace**	mee larshee een parchay
Lie down	**Si metta a terra**	see mayttah ah tayrrah
Listen	**Ascolti**	askoaltee
Listen to me	**Mi ascolti**	mee askoaltee
LOOK	**GUARDI**	gwahrdee
Look out	**Stia attento**	steeah ahttehntoa
POLICE	**POLIZIA**	poaleetseeah
Quick	**Presto**	prehstoa
STOP	**STOP**	stop
Stop here	**Si fermi là**	see fayrmee lah
Stop that man	**Fermate quell'uomo**	fayrmartay kooayllwomoa
Stop thief	**Fermate il ladro**	fayrmartay eel lardroa
Stop or I'll scream	**Si fermi o grido**	see fayrmee o greedoa

FOR CAR ACCIDENTS, see page 150

REFERENCE SECTION

Index

Abbreviations	184	Doctor	162
Airport	65	Drinks	58
Arrival	22	Dry cleaning	126
Baggage	24, 71	Eating out	38
Ballet	82	appetizers	44
Banks	134	cheese	55
Barber's	121	dessert	56
Basic expressions	15	drinks	58
Beach	87	egg dishes	47
Bill	31, 159	fish and seafood	47
Body, parts of	163	fruit	55
Bookshop	104	meat	50
Breakfast	34	pasta, pizza	45
Bus	73	sauces	53
		soups	45
Cables	138	vegetables	54
Camping	89, 106	Electrical appliances	119
Car	142	Emergency	189
accident	150	Filling stations	142
breakdown	151	Games	84
parts	152	Grammar	7
police	150		
rental	26	Hairdressing	121
repair	155	Hotel	25, 28
Casino	85	checking in	29
Change	25	checking out	37
Church services	79	difficulties	35
Cinema	80	registration	32
Clothes	112	service	33
Coach	73	Introductions	92
Colours	113	Invitations	94
Concerts	82		
Customs control	23, 146	Ladies' hairdressing	122
		Laundry	126
Dancing	83	Map	174
Dating	95	Materials	114
Days	181	Measurements	130
Dentist	172	metric	186
Directions	25, 187		

FOR CAR ACCIDENTS, see page 150.

fluids	142
km / miles	144
sizes (clothing)	115
temperature	185
weight	130, 187
Medical section	162
Money	25, 134
Months	182
Motorways	147
Movies	80
Nationalities	175
News-stand	104
Night clubs	83
Numbers	176
Opera	82
Optician	173
Passport control	22, 146
Porters	24, 71
Post-office	137
Pronunciation	12
Provisions	129
Public holidays	183
Questions	78, 100, 144, 180
Railways	66
Records	120
Relaxing	80
Religious services	79
Road signs	
international	160
national	149
Seasons	182
Shopping guide	97
bookshop	104
chemist's	108
clothing	112
colours	113
cosmetics	110
drugstore	108

dry cleaning	126
electrical appliances	119
hairdresser's	121
jeweller's	123
laundry	126
photography	127
provisions	129
records	120
shops, list of	98
tobacconist's	132
toiletry	110
Sightseeing	75
Signs and notices	188
Sizes	115
Snacks	64
Souvenirs	131
Sports	85
Stationer's	104
Subway	72
Taxis	27
Telegrams	138
Telephone	36, 139
Temperature	183, 185
Theatre	81
Time	179
Tire pressure	143
Travel	65
bus	73
car	142
coach	73
plane	65
tickets	69
train	66
tram	73
Underground	72
Voltage	119
Weather	93
Weight	187
Wine	59
Winter sports	88

Quick reference page

Please.	**Per favore.**	pair fah**voaray**
Thank you.	**Grazie.**	**graht**seeay
Yes/No.	**Sì/No.**	see/no
Excuse me.	**Mi scusi.**	mee **skoozee**
Waiter, please.	**Cameriere, per favore.**	kahmayree**ehray** pair fah**voaray**
How much is that?	**Quant'è?**	kwahn**tai**
Where are the toilets?	**Dove sono i gabinetti?**	**doavay soa**noa ee gahbee**nayttee**

Toilets	
SIGNORI/UOMINI (seeñoaree/womeenee)	**SIGNORE/DONNE** (seeñoaray/donnay)

Could you tell me	**Può dirmi...?**	pwo **deermee**
where/when/why	**dove/quando/ perchè**	**doavay/kwahndoa/ pehrkay**
Help me, please.	**Per favore, mi aiuti.**	pair fah**voaray** mee i**ghootee**
Where is the... consulate?	**Dov'è il consolato...?**	doa**vai** eel koansoa**lartoa**
American	**americano**	ahmayree**karnoa**
British	**inglese**	eeng**glayssay**
Canadian	**canadese**	kahnah**dayssay**
What does this mean? I don't understand.	**Cosa significa questo? Non capisco.**	**kaw**sah seeñee**feekah kooaystoa**? noan kah**peeskoa**
Do you speak English?	**Parla inglese?**	**pahrlah** eeng**glayssay**